TEACHER'S PET PUBLICATIONS

LITPLAN TEACHER PACK
for
Homecoming
based on the book by
Cynthia Voigt

Written by
Marion B. Hoffman

© 2000 Teacher's Pet Publications
All Rights Reserved

This **LitPlan** on Cynthia Voigt's **Homecoming**
has been brought to you by Teacher's Pet Publications, Inc.

Copyright Teacher's Pet Publications 2000
11504 Hammock Point
Berlin MD 21811

Only the student materials in this unit plan may be reproduced. Pages such as worksheets and study guides may be reproduced for use in the purchaser's classroom. For any additional copyright questions, contact Teacher's Pet Publications.

www.tpet.com

Table of Contents
Homecoming

Introduction	4
Unit Objectives	8
Unit Outline	9
Reading Assignment Sheet	10
Study Questions (Short Answer)	13
Multiple Choice Quiz Questions	26
Pre-reading Vocabulary Worksheets	55
Lesson One (Introductory Lesson)	73
Nonfiction Assignment Sheet	75
Oral Reading Evaluation Form	76
Writing Assignment #1	83
Writing Assignment #2	91
Writing Assignment #3	97
Vocabulary Review Activities	105
Extra Writing Assignments/Discussion ?s	102
Unit Review Activities	107
Unit Tests	111
Unit Resource Materials	137
Vocabulary Resource Materials	159

Introduction
Homecoming

This unit plan has been carefully designed to give teachers all of the tools they need to present twenty-three daily lessons on Cynthia Voigt's novel, **Homecoming**. All exercises, activities, and assignments in the unit will develop students' reading, writing, thinking, and language skills. In addition to the essential elements, the unit contains a wide variety of extra resource materials and suggested activities.

The **first lesson** uses a bulletin board activity to introduce the theme of what "home" means to different people. All subsequent lessons are designed to maximize the teacher's time while assuring that students at a variety of learning levels are able to progress successfully through the novel.

Reading assignments consist of chapters of the book, beginning with Part I and continuing through Part II. The assignments average twenty-five pages in length. Students do approximately 15 minutes of pre-reading work in conjunction with each reading assignment. Pre-reading involves reviewing the study questions for the assignment and doing some brief vocabulary work connected to the section of reading.

The **study guide questions** are fact based; the answers are right in the text. These questions come in two formats: short answer or multiple choice. It is probably best to use the short answer questions as study guides for students and the multiple choice version for occasional quizzes.

The **vocabulary work** is intended to enrich students' vocabularies and to aid in their understanding of the book. Students will complete a two-part vocabulary worksheet for each section of reading. Part I focuses on students' use of general knowledge and contextual clues by giving the sentence in which the word appears in the text. Students then write down what they think the words mean based on their usage. Part II nails down the definitions of the words by giving students dictionary definitions of the words and asking students to match the words to the correct definitions. There are a total of one hundred vocabulary words in the unit.

Although students can attempt the vocabulary work prior to reading the appropriate section of the book, it is probably best to encourage them to do the vocabulary work while they are reading. Thus the contextual clues that students use in understanding the words would include not just those in the individual quotes but those in sentences surrounding the quote and often in an entire paragraph. By the time that students have finished the reading assignment and completed the companion worksheet, they should have a clear understanding of the meaning of each word.

Students should be encouraged to use the study guide questions to round out their understanding of the text and to prepare for the unit test. The material covered in these questions serves as a way of reviewing the most important events and ideas presented in the reading assignments.

In this unit there is a **Critical Based Questions Option (CQ option)**, which gives the teacher a choice of adding to the fact-based questions some that require more critical thought. These will be found in Lessons Five, Eight, Nine, Eleven, Twelve, and Fifteen. Teachers may use all, some, or none of these optional questions.

There are there **writing assignments** in this unit.

The first assignment, in Lesson Six, asks students to write from personal experience. Students are given two options. They may write about their own lives, mirroring the kinds of information conveyed about the Tillerman children in the novel, or they may write about one of the Tillerman children, explaining why they do or do not admire that character. Either choice will encourage students to examine the text closely and to try to understand the characters better.

The second writing assignment, in Lesson Nine, asks that students write to persuade. The assignment comes at the time that Dicey Tillerman and her family have decided to leave Bridgeport and seek out their grandmother. Students are encouraged to give Dicey advice, (1) to return to Provincetown, (2) to stay in Bridgeport, or (3) to go on to Crisfield to find their grandmother.

The third writing assignment, found in Lesson Thirteen, requires students to write to inform. Just as Dicey Tillerman is good at setting a course and reading maps, students are asked to choose something that they know how to do well and then tell an audience how to do it. Whatever process students choose, they will have to think through all of its steps and then convey the whole process to their audience.

The **nonfiction reading assignment** in this unit focuses on aspects of the area of the Chesapeake Bay and is a precursor to the major class project topic. For the nonfiction assignment, students are given a variety of topics relative to the Chesapeake Bay area and asked to choose one and read about it. After reading their nonfiction pieces, students will fill out a worksheet on which they answer questions regarding facts, interpretation, criticism, and personal opinions. You are also provided with a KWL (What I Know, What I Want To Know, What I Learned) Sheet that may facilitate students' nonfiction reading.

The major **class project** is optional. Project Chesapeake Bay Country is an attempt to get students to move beyond the knowledge they acquire through reading the novel to gain firsthand understanding of a variety of facets of life on or near the Chesapeake Bay. The project is geared to having students discover concerns that need addressing educationally and then to address those concerns in meaningful ways.

You are encouraged to do **group activities** whenever time and circumstances permit. Numerous opportunities are possible for group activities throughout the unit.

Students also will have ample opportunity for **reading aloud** and **making presentations.** Also, a great deal of opportunity will present itself for having rich **class discussions** about the novel and relevant ancillary topics.

One of the most flexible sections of the unit is the **Extra Discussion Questions/Writing Assignments.** In this section you will find interpretive, critical, critical/personal, and personal response questions and quotations from the text that can be used in a number of ways. Some of these questions and quotations are used as the basis for parts of the unit tests.

Review lessons offer chances to review the novel's main events and ideas and to re-examine its characters through **vocabulary review** and **review with games and puzzles**.

The **unit test** comes in five different formats: two different Short Answer Unit Tests, one Advanced Short Answer Unit Test, and two different Multiple Choice Unit Tests. Answer keys are given for all parts of all tests except for the subjective questions that appear in some of the tests.

At the end of Part I of the book is an exercise designed to give you and the students a change of pace through **role playing**.

There are additional **support materials** included with this unit. The **unit resource section** includes suggestions for an in-class library, crossword and word search puzzles related to the novel, and extra vocabulary worksheets. There is a list of **bulletin board ideas** which gives the teacher suggestions for a variety of bulletin boards to supplement the unit. In addition, there is a section called **More Activities** which provides the teacher with even more valuable activities to choose from.

Student materials throughout the unit may be reproduced for use in the teacher's classroom without infringement of copyrights. For a fuller statement of the Teacher's Pet Publications copyright policy, see the back of the title page in this unit.

Author's Notes

One of the first things one notices about **Homecoming** by Cynthia Voigt is her use of a strong, intelligent, and resourceful female protagonist. Dicey Tillerman is a heroine for every season. Not only does she shoulder a lot of responsibility when her mother is around, but she assumes unheard of burdens for a thirteen-year-old once her mother has left the family. She is tough and gentle, serious and funny, and totally honest yet willing to bend the rules just a bit when her family's survival is in question.

When Dicey's mother simply walks away from her four children in the parking lot of a shopping mall, not only do the younger children look to Dicey for guidance and leadership, but she herself steps into her mother's role.

So many burdens are placed on Dicey's shoulders that her character would seem unrealistic were it not for Voigt's ability to present Dicey consistently as a young teenager. She is no adult. But Dicey is a thirteen-year-old girl who faces enormous obstacles and overcomes them one at a time. For the time that she must be in charge, Dicey simply reaches into her incredible depths of maturity, sensitivity, and street smarts and comes out a winner. By the time she has delivered herself and her younger brothers and sister to their grandmother's home in Crisfield, Maryland, Dicey is a strong, courageous, and thoroughly human girl who maintains her own value system and sense of self against almost insurmountable odds.

If your students like **Homecoming,** they're in luck, for it is only the first in a series of books about the Tillerman family. **Dicey's Song**, **A Solitary Blue**, **The Runner**, **Sons from Afar**, and **Seventeen Against the Dealer** are all part of the series.

Voigt received a bachelor's degree from Smith College in 1963. She taught high school English for a couple of years in Maryland and later taught and was department chair at The Key School in Annapolis, Maryland. Born in 1942, she currently lives with her family and their dog in Maine. Some of her other books are **Tell Me if the Lovers are Losers**, **The Callender Papers**, **Building Blocks, Jackaroo, Izzy, Willy-Nilly**, **Tree by Leaf**, and **On Fortune's Wheel.**

A great deal of information about this prolific writer is available both in print and via the internet. I encourage you to have your students seek out information on the author as well as to read her other books. **Homecoming** was, after all, only her first novel. More enjoyment lies ahead.

Unit Objectives
Homecoming

1. Through reading **Homecoming** by Cynthia Voigt, students will gain a better understanding of a variety of themes, such as what makes a home, friendship, family ties, love, mental illness, and religion.. The themes in the book are almost too numerous to mention.

2. Students will demonstrate their understanding of the text on four levels: factual, interpretive, critical, and personal.

3. Students will define their own viewpoints on the vast number of issues presented in the novel.

4. Students will be exposed to new ways of looking at their own lives and the lives of other people.

5. Students will study various aspects of modern farming and will create plans for dealing with some of the needs of the farming community.

6. Students will be practice reading aloud as well as silently.

7. Students will enrich their vocabularies and improve their understanding of the novel through the vocabulary lessons prepared for use in conjunction with it.

8. Students will practice writing through a variety of assignments.

9. The writing assignments in this unit are geared to several purposes:
    a. to check the students' reading comprehension
    b. to make students think about the ideas presented in the book
    c. to allow students to write from personal experience, to inform, and to persuade
    d. to provide the opportunity to review standard English
    e. to encourage critical and logical thinking

10. Students will be encouraged to make connections between the book and real life.

Unit Outline
Homecoming

1 Introduction Distribution of materials	2 PVR I 1 & 2 Oral reading assignment and evaluation	3 PVR I 3 & 4 Character discussion	4 Nonfiction Reading Assignment	5 PVR I 5 & 6 Report fact on NFRA Assign I 7 & 8 CQ option
6 Check work for I 7 & 8 or do in class WA #1 (pers exp)	7 Finish WA #1 if necessary Quiz on 1st 8 chapters PVR I 9	8 PVR I 10 & 11 Start optional class project CQ option	9 PVR I 12 WA #2 (persuade) CQ option	10 END BOOK PART I Role playing exercise
11 Quiz on Part I of the book PVR II 1 & 2 CQ option	12 PVR II 3 & 4 Project updates or Theme/character discussion CQ option	13 PRV II 5 & 6 WA #3 (inform)	14 Finish WA #3 PVR II 7	15 PVR II 8 Quiz on last 7 chapters CQ option
16 PVR II 9 & 10 Discussion of characters in the book	17 Quiz on whole book to date Review of ideas and	18 PVR II 11 & 12 Brief review	19 Review with Extra Discussion Questions/Writing Assignments	20 More review with Extra Questions or use of suggested variations
21 Vocabulary review	22 Review with games and activities	23 Unit Tests		

Reading Assignment Sheet

Section of the Text	Date Assigned	Date Completed
BOOK PART I		
Chapters 1 & 2		
Chapters 3 & 4		
Chapters 5 & 6		
Chapters 7 & 8		
Chapter 9		
Chapters 10 & 11		
Chapter 12		
BOOK PART II		
Chapters 1 & 2		
Chapters 3 & 4		
Chapters 5 & 6		
Chapter 7		
Chapter 8		
Chapters 9 & 10		
Chapters 11 & 12		

STUDY QUESTIONS

Short Answer Questions
Homecoming

Part I Chapters 1 & 2
1. Where did Dicey's mother leave her three children?
2. Why was the Tillerman family traveling to Bridgeport?
3. What does the guard at the mall think Dicey has done wrong?
4. Why was Dicey able to outrun the guard?
5. What was the first thing James said when he woke up in the car in the morning?
6. How long did Dicey estimate it would take to walk to Bridgeport?
7. Who finally persuades Sammy to start walking to Bridgeport?
8. What did the police investigate as the children first started walking?
9. Who is always arguing with Dicey's decisions?
10. What does Dicey discover when they are near Stonington?

Part I Chapters 3 & 4
1. What did the children at the public beach that made cooking chicken and potatoes possible?
2. Where is the children's father?
3. What story does Dicey totally make up about her parents.
4. What does Dicey learn that makes her understand why Sammy became less happy as he started to grow?
5. Who is Peggy-o?
6. What did the children eat steamed at Rockland State Park?
7. Who are Lou and Edie?
8. What did Lou and Edie do that was against the law?
9. What accident did James have at Rockland State Park?
10. How did Sammy's persistence pay off at Rockland State Park?

Part I Chapters 5 & 6
1. Why do the children stay so long at Rockland?
2. What does Sammy do at Rockland that is wrong?
3. How did Dicey decide the world was arranged that made it tough for kids?
4. What do both the mall guard and Lou and Edie believe about Dicey?
5. What did Sammy bring back to the campsite that Dicey made him return?
6. How did Dicey make some money to buy a map in Sound View?
7. What discovery at Old Lyme nearly brought Dicey to tears?
8. How did the Tillermans make money outside the grocery store?
9. Where did the children sleep after rowing across the river?
10. What does James say is the only true, unchanging thing?

Short Answer Questions continued page 2

Part I Chapters 7 & 8
1. Who did the children meet on the college campus in New Haven?
2. What state is Provincetown in?
3. What did all of the Tillerman children get to do in the dormitory room when they awoke?
4. What did James do in the dormitory room that made Dicey feel ashamed?
5. What mannerism about Windy did Dicey notice most?
6. What song did Maybeth sing with Stewart?
7. What did Stewart and the children do in Fairfield before going to Bridgeport?
8. How did the Tillermans arrive in Bridgeport?

Part I Chapters 9 & 10
1. What did the Tillermans learn about Aunt Cilla when they met Cousin Eunice?
2. What is Cousin Eunice's full name?
3. Who did Cousin Eunice call on for help?
4. What emotion did Dicey say that Cousin Eunice felt for the Tillerman children?
5. What was Dicey's biggest disappointment about the location of Aunt Cilla's house?
6. What does Dicey learn from Cousin Eunice about her grandmother, Abigail Tillerman?
7. What does Father Joseph ask Dicey if she is willing to do?
8. What words did Dicey go to bed reciting to herself?

Part I Chapters 10 & 11
1. What does Cousin Eunice do every morning at 6:30?
2. Why does James like the school at the day camp in Bridgeport?
3. What does Cousin Eunice do at her job?
4. What kind of an expression did Dicey's grandmother wear in Cousin Eunice's picture album?
5. What is the name of Dicey's long missing father?
6. Why did the Police Department of Peewauket send Dicey fifty-seven dollars?
7. What kind of job did Dicey get in Bridgeport?
8. What word does Father Joseph apply to Maybeth in his discussion with Dicey?
9. Who is doing all of the work in and around Cousin Eunice's house?
10. What is Cousin Eunice's reason for saying that she must abandon becoming a nun?

Part I Chapter 12
1. What does Sister Bernenice suggest to Dicey about Maybeth?
2. What big problem is Sammy causing at the summer school camp?
3. After picking her brothers and sisters up from camp, what does Dicey decide to do?
4. What news does Sergeant Gordo bring about Dicey's mother?
5. Who is Dicey planning to take to Crisfield with her?
6. What is the result of James' discovery of Dicey's Crisfield plans?

Short Answer Questions continued page 3

Part II Chapters 1 & 2
1. What does Dicey figure was the expense of staying with Cousin Eunice?
2. What decision of Dicey's disappointed James.
3. Who did the children meet down at the Annapolis boatyard?
4. How do the Tillermans expect to get to the Eastern Shore?

Part II Chapters 3 & 4
1. On reflection, what does Dicey think she started thinking the wrong way at Cousin Eunice's?
2. Why is Dicey so personally happy when they are sailing toward the Eastern Shore?
3. What does Jerry allow Dicey to do on the boat?
4. What does Jerry say Tom always tries to get him to do?
5. Where did Jerry and Tom drop the Tillermans off?
6. What did Dicey recognize in the voice of the storekeeper in St. Michael's?
7. What did the children recognize in the looks of the young people on the Eastern Shore?
8. Who did the children meet at the circus in Easton?

Part II Chapters 5 & 6
1. What do the children decide to do to make some money?
2. Why wouldn't Dicey agree to leave even when she felt uneasy about Mr. Rudyard?
3. How did Mr. Rudyard keep the children in the field even after Dicey said they had to leave?
4. What diverted the dog's attention from tracking the children?
5. How did the children escape from Mr. Rudyard?
6. How did Mr. Rudyard continue to pursue the Tillermans?
7. Who saved the children from Mr. Rudyard?
8. What did Mr. Rudyard try to claim?
9. Who personally ran Mr. Rudyard off?

Part II Chapter 7
1. How did the children get to Crisfield?
2. What assurance did Will give the children before leaving them?
3. What did Dicey tell the woman in the Crisfield store about why she was looking for Abigail Tillerman?
4. What was the word that occurred to Dicey to describe her first view of her grandmother's farm?
5. Where did Dicey finally find her grandmother?
6. What does Dicey quote when her grandmother asks what she thinks of death?
7. Why does Dicey's grandmother say she is glad her husband died?

Short Answer Questions continued page 4

Part II Chapter 8
1. How did her grandmother surprise Dicey just as Dicey was turning to leave?
2. How did her grandmother know who Dicey was?
3. What does her grandmother finally offer the family?
4. How did Dicey and her grandmother get back to Crisfield.
5. What happened when Dicey returned to Crisfield for her three siblings?
6. How did James and Maybeth get to the farm from town?
7. Why was Dicey upset with James?
8. What surprising thing did Dicey find out in the barn?
9. What decision does Dicey make about her grandmother's house?
10. What did the Tillerman children first learn to eat at their grandmother's house?

Part II Chapters 9 & 10
1. What question about her grandmother did Dicey start trying to answer the first morning there?
2. What project did the children choose for their first day at their grandmother's house?
3. What did the children's grandmother say her husband did with books?
4. What presents did the children receive when Will and Claire visited the farm?
5. What did her grandmother respond when Dicey asked if she expected the children to stay?

Part II Chapters 11 & 12
1. What did Dicey and her grandmother talk about privately in the kitchen late at night?
2. What had their grandmother decided by the next morning about the children's future?
3. What did the Tillermans and their grandmother do at the school the next morning?
4. What was Maybeth's major accomplishment of the day?
5. How did the children's grandmother introduce them to the woman in the grocery store?
6. What major concession does the children's grandmother make at the dock?
7. What special question did Dicey ask her grandmother?
8. What important question did the children's grandmother ask just before they left the dock?

Key: Short Answer Questions Homecoming

Part I Chapters 1 & 2

1. Where did Dicey's mother leave her three children?
   She left them in a car in a shopping mall parking lot.

2. Why was the Tillerman family traveling to Bridgeport?
   They were going to Aunt Cilla's house for help.

3. What does the guard at the mall think Dicey has done wrong?
   He thinks that she broke a window at Record City.

4. Why was Dicey able to outrun the guard?
   He was out of shape and overweight.

5. What was the first thing James said when he woke up in the car in the morning?
   He said, "It's still true."

6. How long did Dicey estimate it would take to walk to Bridgeport?
   She estimated two or three days.

7. Who finally persuades Sammy to start walking to Bridgeport?
   Maybeth persuades him.

8. What did the police investigate as the children first started walking?
   The police investigated the abandoned car.

9. Who is always arguing with Dicey's decisions?
   Sammy is.

10. What does Dicey discover when they are near Stonington?
    She discovers that the trip is going to take much longer than she originally thought.

Part I Chapters 3 & 4

1. What did the children discover at the public beach that made cooking chicken and potatoes possible?
   They found three picnic shelters with stone fireplaces in them for cooking.

2. Where is the children's father?
   Their father left the family years earlier.

3. What story does Dicey totally make up about her parents.
   She pretends that they were married.

4. What does Dicey learn that makes her understand why Sammy became less happy as he started to grow?
   She learns that the other children at school teased him about his mother and Maybeth.

5. Who is Peggy-o?
   She is a character in a song that the children's mother taught them.

6. What did the children eat steamed at Rockland State Park?
   They ate mussels and clams.

7. Who are Lou and Edie?
   They are the two teenage runaways that the children met at Rockland State Park.

8. What did Lou and Edie do that was against the law?
   They stole money from Edie's father.

9. What accident did James have at Rockland State Park?
   He fell from the top of a rounded boulder.

10. How did Sammy's persistence pay off at Rockland State Park?
    He caught three fish.

Part I Chapters 5 & 6

1. Why do the children stay so long at Rockland?
   They stay while James recuperates from a fall.

2. What does Sammy do at Rockland that is wrong?
   He steals a picnic lunch.

3. How did Dicey decide the world was arranged that made it tough for kids?
   She decided the world was arranged for adults who had money.

4. What do both the mall guard and Lou and Edie believe about Dicey?
   They all believe she is a boy named Danny.

5. What did Sammy bring back to the campsite that Dicey made him return?
   Sammy brought a wallet with twenty dollars in it.

6. How did Dicey make some money to buy a map in Sound View?
   She washed the windows at the Texaco station.

7. What discovery at Old Lyme nearly brought Dicey to tears?
   She learned that the bridge across the river had no walkway.

8. How did the Tillermans make money outside the grocery store?
   They carried customers' bags of groceries to their cars.

9. Where did the children sleep after rowing across the river?
   They slept in a cemetery.

10. What does James say is the only true, unchanging thing?
    He says it is the speed of light.

Part I Chapters 7 & 8
1. Who did the children meet on the college campus in New Haven?
   They met Windy and his roommate Stewart.

2. What state is Provincetown in?
   The town is in Massachusetts.

3. What did all of the Tillerman children get to do in the dormitory room when they awoke?
   They all got to have a shower.

4. What did James do in the dormitory room that made Dicey feel ashamed?
   James stole money from Stewart.

5. What mannerism about Windy did Dicey notice most?
   She noticed that his eyebrows and moustache seemed to move with a life of their own.

6. What song did Maybeth sing with Stewart?
   She sang Greensleeves.

7. What did Stewart and the children do in Fairfield before going to Bridgeport?
   They ate at McDonald's and bought a map.

8. How did the Tillermans arrive in Bridgeport?
   Stewart drove them there.

Part I Chapter 9

1. What did the Tillermans learn about Aunt Cilla when they met Cousin Eunice?
   They learned that Aunt Cilla had died.

2. What is Cousin Eunice's full name?
   It is Miss Eunice Logan.

3. Who did Cousin Eunice call on for help?
   She called on Father Joseph, her friend and spiritual counselor.

4. What emotion did Dicey say that Cousin Eunice felt for the Tillerman children?
   Dicey said she felt pity.

5. What was Dicey's biggest disappointment about the location of Aunt Cilla's house?
   Her biggest disappointment was that it wasn't near the ocean.

6. What does Dicey learn from Cousin Eunice about her grandmother, Abigail Tillerman?
   She learns that her grandmother lives in Crisfield on the Eastern Shore of Maryland.

7. What does Father Joseph ask Dicey if she is willing to do?
   He asks if she is willing to talk with the police.

8. What words did Dicey go to bed reciting to herself?
   She recited Crisfield, Eastern Shore, Maryland.

Part I Chapters 10 & 11

1. What does Cousin Eunice do every morning at 6:30?
   She goes to mass.

2. Why does James like the school at the day camp in Bridgeport?
   He likes the chance to learn from the priests.

3. What does Cousin Eunice do at her job?
   She is a junior foreman at a factory where she and her crew sew lacy insets into lingerie.

4. What kind of an expression did Dicey's grandmother wear in Cousin Eunice's picture album?
   She wore a sour expression.

5. What is the name of Dicey's long missing father?
   His name is Francis Verricker.

6. Why did the Police Department of Peewauket send Dicey fifty-seven dollars?
   It was for the sale of her mother's car.

7. What kind of job did Dicey get in Bridgeport?
   She got a job washing dirty windows on neighborhood stores.

8. What word does Father Joseph apply to Maybeth in his discussion with Dicey?
   He uses the word "retarded."

9. Who is doing all of the work in and around Cousin Eunice's house?
   Dicey is.

10. What is Cousin Eunice's reason for saying that she must abandon becoming a nun?
    She says that her duty is to the abandoned Tillerman children.

Part I Chapter 12
1. What does Sister Berenice suggest to Dicey about Maybeth?
   Sister Berenice thinks that Maybeth should be in a special school for the disabled.

2. What big problem is Sammy causing at the summer school camp?
   Sammy is fighting all the time.

3. After picking her brothers and sisters up from camp, what does Dicey decide to do?
   She decides to go to Crisfield to meet her grandmother.

4. What news does Sergeant Gordo bring about Dicey's mother?
   She is in a catatonic state in a mental hospital in Massachusetts.

5. Who is Dicey planning to take to Crisfield with her?
   She is planning to go by herself.

6. What is the result of James' discovery of Dicey's Crisfield plans?
   The result is that all of the Tillermans leave Bridgeport for Crisfield, Maryland.

Part II Chapters 1 & 2
1. What does Dicey figure was the expense of staying with Cousin Eunice?
   She figures it is the cost of always being grateful.

2. What decision of Dicey's disappointed James.
   She left a note telling Cousin Eunice where they were heading.

3. Who did the children meet down at the Annapolis boatyard?
   They met Jerry and Tom.

4. How do the Tillermans expect to get to the Eastern Shore?
   They talk Jerry and Tom into taking them there on Jerry's father's boat.

Part II Chapters 3 & 4
1. On reflection, why does Dicey think she started thinking the wrong way at Cousin Eunice's?
   She thinks it is because the children were separated and didn't do things together.

2. Why is Dicey so personally happy when they are sailing toward the Eastern Shore?
   She is happy because she is on the water.

3. What does Jerry allow Dicey to do on the boat?
   He allows her to steer it.

4. What does Jerry say Tom always tries to do to him?
   He says that Tom always tries to get him into trouble.

5. Where did Jerry and Tom drop the Tillermans off?
   They dropped them off at St. Michael's.

6. What did Dicey recognize in the voice of the storekeeper in St. Michael's?
   She recognized that the clerk sounded a little like her mother.

7. What did the children recognize in the looks of the young people on the Eastern Shore?
   They recognized their own likeness.

8. Who did the children meet at the circus in Easton?
   They met Claire and Will.

Part II Chapters 5 & 6
1. What do the children decide to do to make some money?
   They decide to become tomato pickers.

2. Why wouldn't Dicey agree to leave even when she felt uneasy about Mr. Rudyard?
   She wouldn't leave because they hadn't been paid yet.

3. How did Mr. Rudyard keep the children in the field even after Dicey said they had to leave?
   He threatened them with his dog.

4. What diverted the dog's attention from tracking the children?
   The dog stopped to eat the leftover biscuits.

5. How did the children escape from Mr. Rudyard?
   They swam down the river.

6. How did Mr. Rudyard continue to pursue the Tillermans?
   He drove after them in his pickup truck and then ran after them on foot with his dog.

7. Who saved the children from Mr. Rudyard?
   The people with the circus did.

8. What did Mr. Rudyard try to claim?
   He tried to claim that the Tillermans were his foster children.

9. Who personally ran Mr. Rudyard off?
   Claire did.

Part II Chapter 7

1. How did the children get to Crisfield?
   Will drove them there.

2. What assurance did Will give the children before leaving them?
   Will said that they could always call on him for help.

3. What did Dicey tell the woman in the Crisfield store about why she was looking for Abigail Tillerman?
   Dicey told the woman that she wanted to work on the farm.

4. What was the word that occurred to Dicey to describe her first view of her grandmother's farm?
   The word that occurred to her was "abandoned."

5. Where did Dicey finally find her grandmother?
   She was sitting out on the back steps.

6. What does Dicey quote when her grandmother asks what she thinks of death?
   Dicey quotes what she had read earlier on the tombstone about being home from the hill

and the sea.

7. Why does Dicey's grandmother say she is glad her husband died?
She says he always wanted her to polish his shoes instead of polishing them himself.

Part II Chapter 8
1. How did her grandmother surprise Dicey just as Dicey was turning to leave?
Her grandmother said that she knew who Dicey was and that Dicey couldn't stay there.

2. How did her grandmother know who Dicey was?
She knew because she had received a letter from Cousin Eunice in Bridgeport.

3. What does her grandmother finally offer the family?
She offers to let them sleep there for one night.

4. How did Dicey and her grandmother get back to Crisfield.
They traveled in her grandmother's boat.

5. What happened when Dicey returned to Crisfield for her three siblings?
Only Sammy had waited there for her.

6. How did James and Maybeth get to the farm from town?
They walked.

7. Why was Dicey upset with James?
She was upset because she had told him to wait for her with the younger children.

8. What surprising thing did Dicey find out in the barn?
She found a sailboat.

9. What decision does Dicey make about her grandmother's house?
Dicey decides that the farm is the right place for her and her siblings.

10. What did the Tillerman children first learn to eat at their grandmother's house?
They learned to eat crabs.

Part II Chapters 9 & 10
1. What question about her grandmother did Dicey start trying to answer the first morning there?
She wanted to know what her grandmother was like inside, not just outside.

2. What project did the children choose for their first day at their grandmother's house?
They decided to pull down the honeysuckle vines.

3. What did the children's grandmother say her husband did with books?
She said he used his books to build a wall to keep things out.

4. What presents did the children receive when Will and Claire visited the farm?
The children each received a bicycle.

5. What did her grandmother respond when Dicey asked if she expected the children to stay?
Her grandmother said no.

Part II Chapters 11 & 12

1. What did Dicey and her grandmother talk about privately in the kitchen late at night?
They talked about the past—her grandmother's and her mother's.

2. What had their grandmother decided by the next morning about the children's future?
She had decided to let them stay with her until Cousin Eunice had responded to her letter.

3. What did the Tillermans and their grandmother do at the school the next morning?
They got the children registered for school in Crisfield.

4. What was Maybeth's major accomplishment of the day?
Maybeth stayed by herself for testing and was good enough to get placed in third grade.

5. How did the children's grandmother introduce them to the woman in the grocery store?
She introduced them as her grandchildren.

6. What major concession does the children's grandmother make at the dock?
She says that the children can stay with her.

7. What special question did Dicey ask her grandmother?
She asked if she could fix the sailboat up and have it.

8. What important question did the children's grandmother ask just before they left the dock?
She asked if they were ready to go home.

Multiple Choice Questions
Homecoming

Part I Chapters 1 & 2

1. Where did Dicey's mother leave her three children?
    a. She left them with a babysitter.
    b. She left them with strangers.
    c. She left them in a car in a shopping mall parking lot.
    d. She left them with their grandparents.

2. Why was the Tillerman family traveling to Bridgeport?
    a. They had just bought a new home there.
    b. Dicey thought her father might be living there.
    c. Dicey's mother had some good friends there.
    d. They were going to Aunt Cilla's house for help.

3. What does the guard at the mall think Dicey has done wrong?
    a. He thinks she is a thief.
    b. He thinks she has run away from home.
    c. He thinks that she broke a window at Record City.
    d. He thinks she is part of a gambling ring in town.

4. Why was Dicey able to outrun the guard?
    a. Because she knew the town better than he did
    b. Because he was out of shape and overweight
    c. Just because she was young
    d. Because she was smarter than he

5. What was the first thing James said when he woke up in the car in the morning?
    a. He said, "Oh no, not another long day."
    b. He said, "Dicey, please get us some food."
    c. He said, "It's still true."
    d. He said, "Do you think our mother will return today>"

6. How long did Dicey estimate it would take to walk to Bridgeport?
    a. About six months
    b. Two or three days
    c. Six hours
    d. At least a year

Multiple Choice Quizzes continued page 2

7. Who finally persuades Sammy to start walking to Bridgeport?
   a. Dicey
   b. Maybeth
   c. James
   d. A police officer

8. What did the police investigate as the children first started walking?
   a. The children's juvenile records
   b. Their own consciences
   c. Their car engines
   d. The abandoned car

9. Who is always arguing with Dicey's decisions?
   a. Sammy
   b. Maybeth
   c. The children at school
   d. Edie and Lou

10. What does Dicey discover when they are near Stonington?
    a. That the trip is going to take much longer than she originally thought
    b. That she had thrown her map away with the leftovers from lunch
    c. That walking is really tough
    d. That she should have come on her own

Multiple Choice Quizzes continued page 3

<u>Part I Chapters 3 & 4</u>
1. What did the children discover at the public beach that made cooking chicken and potatoes possible?
    a. They found three picnic shelters with stone fireplaces in them for cooking.
    b. They came upon an old campfire in the wooded area of the beach.
    c. They realized that they had some matches with them.
    d. They realized that Dicey had brought some chicken recipes.

2. Where is the children's father?
    a. He left them years earlier.
    b. He is living in New York City.
    c. He died just before Maybeth was born.
    d. He lives with his new family in Georgia.

3. What story does Dicey totally make up about her parents.
    a. That they once won the lottery
    b. That they were married
    c. That they met in a romantic place
    d. That they used to hug and kiss all the time

4. What does Dicey learn that makes her understand why Sammy became less happy as he started to grow?
    a. That he really started learning the truth about life
    b. That he was never happy after having a major illness
    c. That he couldn't stay happy with a crazy mother
    d. That the other children at school teased him about his mother and Maybeth

5. Who is Peggy-o?
    a, The children's mother's best friend
    b. A character in a song that the children's mother taught them
    c. The children's mother's sister
    d. A friend from the Tillermans' old neighborhood

6. What did the children eat steamed at Rockland State Park?
    a. Crabs
    b. Rice
    c. Catfish
    d. Mussels and clams

Multiple Choice Quizzes continued page 4

7. Who are Lou and Edie?
    a. Two singers the children enjoy listening to
    b. Their parents
    c. Two teenage runaways that the children met at Rockland State Park
    d. Two of their father's close friends

8. What did Lou and Edie do that was against the law?
    a. They got married.
    b. They stole money from Edie's father.
    c. They killed someone.
    d. They held up a grocery store.

9. What accident did James have at Rockland State Park?
    a. He nearly drowned.
    b. He hurt himself with a stick of dynamite.
    c. He fell from the top of a rounded boulder.
    d. He broke his leg falling into the lake.

10. How did Sammy's persistence pay off at Rockland State Park?
    a. He made Dicey change her mind about leaving.
    b. He caught three fish.
    c. He got all three of the other children to agree to go fishing.
    d. He made James promise not to holler at him.

Multiple Choice Quizzes continued page 5

Part I Chapters 5 & 6

1. Why do the children stay so long at Rockland?
    a. Because it is so beautiful there
    b. Because Dicey can't make up her mind which way to go next
    c. Because Maybeth gets sick
    d. Because James is recuperating from a fall

2. What does Sammy do at Rockland that is wrong?
    a. He catches fish illegally.
    b. He steals a picnic lunch.
    c. He sasses Dicey.
    d. He runs off for hours at a time by himself.

3. How did Dicey decide the world was arranged that made it tough for kids?
    a. She decided that the world was arranged for adults who had money.
    b. She decided that kids were hampered by their lack of height.
    c. She realized that most adults disliked children.
    d. She realized that most children were too dumb to make it in the world.

4. What do both the mall guard and Lou and Edie believe about Dicey?
    a. That she is a thief
    b. That she is pretty smart
    c. That she is a boy named Danny
    d. That her mother is returning soon

5. What did Sammy bring back to the campsite that Dicey made him return?
    a. Two cheese sandwiches
    b. A wallet with twenty dollars in it
    c. A small brown dog
    d. An ID card that he found nearby

6. How did Dicey make some money to buy a map in Sound View?
    a. She washed the windows at the Texaco station.
    b. She handed out leaflets all over town.
    c. She swept up in the local grocery store.
    d. She sold cookies.

Multiple Choice Quizzes continued page 6

7. What discovery at Old Lyme nearly brought Dicey to tears?
    a. She learned that the bridge across the river had no walkway.
    b. She learned that they were completely out of doughnuts.
    c. She learned that she had made a wrong turn ten miles before.
    d. She learned that she had always been mean to Sammy.

8. How did the Tillermans make money outside the grocery store?
    a. They begged for it.
    b. They washed the store windows.
    c. They sold cookies.
    d. They carried customers' bags of groceries to their cars.

9. Where did the children sleep after rowing across the river?
    a. They slept in an abandoned house.
    b. They slept in a church.
    c. They slept in a cemetery.
    d. They slept in an open meadow.

10. What does James say is the only true, unchanging thing?
    a. The speed of light
    b. His mother's love for him
    c. His intellect
    d. His belief in God

Multiple Choice Quizzes continued page 7

Part I Chapters 7 & 8

1. Who did the children meet on the college campus in New Haven?
    a. Some traveling musicians
    b. A bunch of circus people
    c. Windy and his roommate Stewart
    d. An old friend of their mother's

2. What state is Provincetown in?
    a. Georgia
    b. Massachusetts
    c. Minnesota
    d. Colorado

3. What did all of the Tillerman children get to do in the dormitory room when they awoke?
    a. They got to order some food from a fast food restaurant.
    b. They got to meet all of Windy and Stewart's friends.
    c. They got to tell the stories of their adventures.
    d. They got to have a shower.

4. What did James do in the dormitory room that made Dicey feel ashamed?
    a. He yelled at Windy.
    b. He told lies to everyone.
    c. He refused to help clean up the room.
    d. He stole money from Stewart.

5. What mannerism about Windy did Dicey notice most?
    a. His eyebrows and moustache seemed to move with a life of their own.
    b. He winced a lot.
    c. He had wonderfully straight teeth.
    d. He talked without moving his mouth.

6. What song did Maybeth sing with Stewart?
    a. The one about Peggy-o
    b. Greensleeves
    c. A hymn
    d. Pretty Girl of Mine

Multiple Choice Quizzes continued page 8

7. What did Stewart and the children do in Fairfield before going to Bridgeport?
   a. They ate at McDonald's and bought a map.
   b. They swam in the ocean.
   c. They stopped in a nearby church and prayed for their mother.
   d. They met some street musicians.

8. How did the Tillermans arrive in Bridgeport?
   a. Stewart drove them there.
   b. They walked.
   c. They took the bus.
   d. They rode in a taxicab.

Multiple Choice Quizzes continued page 9

Part I Chapters 9

1. What did the Tillermans learn about Aunt Cilla when they met Cousin Eunice?
    a. That she was gravely ill
    b. That she had died
    c. That she wasn't even their real aunt
    d. That she was out of town

2. What is Cousin Eunice's full name?
    a. Mrs. Eunice Kaminsky
    b. Miss Eunice Logan
    c. Ms. Eunice Tillerman
    d. Miss Eunice Hallohan

3. Who did Cousin Eunice call on for help?
    a. Her mother
    b. Father Joseph
    c. Her next-door-neighbor
    d. Sister Berenice

4. What emotion did Dicey say that Cousin Eunice felt for the Tillerman children?
    a. Love
    b. Sympathy
    c. Empathy
    d. Pity

5. What was Dicey's biggest disappointment about the location of Aunt Cilla's house?
    a. It was too far from the mall.
    b. It wasn't near the ocean.
    c. It was located in a bad neighborhood.
    d. It was right off a major highway.

6. What does Dicey learn from Cousin Eunice about her grandmother, Abigail Tillerman?
    a. That her grandmother has died
    b. That her grandmother was too ill to see anyone
    c. That her grandmother lives in Crisfield on the Eastern Shore of Maryland
    d. That her grandmother had just moved out of the United States

Multiple Choice Quizzes continued page 10

7. What does Father Joseph ask Dicey if she is willing to do?
    a. He asks if she is willing to talk with the police.
    b. He asks if she is willing to become a nun.
    c. He asks if the children are willing to change their last name.
    d. He asks if she is willing to become a Catholic.

8. What words did Dicey go to bed reciting to herself?
    a. No way. We're not splitting up.
    b. We have to make it.
    c. Crisfield, Eastern Shore, Maryland
    d. Cousin Eunice is so nice.

Multiple Choice Quizzes continued page 11

Part I Chapters 10 & 11
1. What does Cousin Eunice do every morning at 6:30?
    a. She says a prayer for her mother.
    b. She goes to mass.
    c. She phones her mother.
    d. She leaves to go to work.

2. Why does James like the school at the day camp in Bridgeport?
    a. Because it is located in a really nice neighborhood
    b. Because he likes the chance to learn from the priests
    c. Because they have horseback riding there
    d. Because he gets to study Latin there

3. What does Cousin Eunice do at her job?
    a. She is a school crossing guard.
    b. She teaches elementary school.
    c. She is a junior foreman in a factory
    d. She is a church official

4. What kind of an expression did Dicey's grandmother wear in Cousin Eunice's picture album?
    a. A huge smile
    b. A timid expression
    c. A puzzled look
    d. A sour expression

5. What is the name of Dicey's long missing father?
    a. Eric Francois
    b. Louis Lamour
    c. Francis Verricker
    d. Samuel Tillerman

6. Why did the Police Department of Peewauket send Dicey fifty-seven dollars?
    a. They took up a fund to help the children out.
    b. It was for the sale of her mother's car.
    c. It was money they confiscated when the abandoned car was found.
    d. It was money that was stolen from Dicey in the shopping mall.

Multiple Choice Quizzes continued page 12

7. What kind of job did Dicey get in Bridgeport?
   a. She washed store windows.
   b. She babysat younger children.
   c. She sold cookies.
   d. She handed out leaflets on the street.

8. What word does Father Joseph apply to Maybeth in his discussion with Dicey?
   a. Retarded
   b. Cute
   c. Conniving
   d. A little wicked

9. Who is doing all of the work in and around Cousin Eunice's house?
   a. Cousin Eunice
   b. Cousin Eunice's old housekeeper
   c. Dicey
   d. A cleaning service

10. What is Cousin Eunice's reason for saying that she must abandon becoming a nun?
    a. Because she really doesn't have a calling
    b. Because her duty is to the abandoned Tillerman children
    c. Because her mother wouldn't have wanted her to do it
    d. Because she is too old

Multiple Choice Quizzes continued page 13

Part I Chapter 12
1. What does Sister Berenice suggest to Dicey about Maybeth?
    a. She thinks that Maybeth should be in a special school for the disabled.
    b. She thinks that Maybeth should be in third grade.
    c. She thinks Maybeth is really an adopted child.
    d. She thinks Maybeth is one of the sweetest children she has ever met.

2. What big problem is Sammy causing at the summer school camp?
    a. He swears all the time.
    b. He is fighting all the time.
    c. He is a bully.
    d. He is a little retarded.

3. After picking her brothers and sisters up from camp, what does Dicey decide to do?
    a. She decides to leave them all in camp because they are so happy.
    b. She decides to go to Crisfield to meet her grandmother.
    c. She decides to return to Peewaukit and wait for her mother.
    d. She decides that she herself wants to attend the camp.

4. What news does Sergeant Gordo bring about Dicey's mother?
    a. That her mother has been found dead
    b. That her mother is back home in Provincetown
    c. That her mother is in a catatonic state in a mental hospital in Massachusetts
    d. That his investigation shows that her mother is living in Maryland

5. Who is Dicey planning to take to Crisfield with her?
    a. Only James because he is so smart
    b. No one
    c. Maybeth because she can't leave her alone
    d. Sammy because he is the youngest child

6. What is the result of James' discovery of Dicey's Crisfield plans?
    a. All the Tillermans leave Bridgeport for Crisfield, Maryland
    b. He steals some of her money and the map.
    c. He yells at her and calls her names.
    d. He packs and returns to Provincetown.

Multiple Choice Quizzes continued page 14

Part II Chapters 1 & 2
1. What does Dicey figure was the expense of staying with Cousin Eunice?
   a. Nearly a hundred dollars
   b. Her loss of pride
   c. The cost of always being grateful
   d. Her dignity

2. What decision of Dicey's disappointed James.
   a. She left a note telling Cousin Eunice where they were heading.
   b. She told Cousin Eunice the truth.
   c. She lied to the police.
   d. She said she was giving up on finding their mother.

3. Who did the children meet down at the Annapolis boatyard?
   a. Edie and Louis
   b. An old friend of their father's
   c. Will and Claire
   d. Jerry and Tom

4. How do the Tillermans expect to get to the Eastern Shore?
   a. They talk Jerry and Tom into taking them there on Jerry's father's boat.
   b. They decide to walk.
   c. They decide to try taking the bus.
   d. They decide to get Will and Claire to take them.

Multiple Choice Quizzes continued page 15

Part II Chapters 3 & 4

1. On reflection, why does Dicey think she started thinking the wrong way at Cousin Eunice's?
   a. She should never have listened to Cousin Eunice.
   b. The children were separated and didn't do things together.
   c. She got too involved with the camp school.
   d. She got confused by Father Joseph.

2. Why is Dicey so personally happy when they are sailing toward the Eastern Shore?
   a. Because she really disliked Cousin Eunice
   b. Because her mother taught her songs about the Eastern Shore
   c. Because she is happy that she is on the water
   d. Because the other children are happy on the boat

3. What does Jerry allow Dicey to do on the boat?
   a. He gives her some beer.
   b. He allows her to steer it.
   c. He allows her how to plot their course.
   d. He allows her to swim off the side of the boat.

4. What does Jerry say Tom always tries to do to him?
   a. Pull practical tricks on him
   b. Get him to move out of his parents' home
   c. Get him to feel good about himself
   d. Get him into trouble

5. Where did Jerry and Tom drop the Tillermans off?
   a. In the middle of Provincetown
   b. At St. Michael's
   c. Just outside of Crisfield
   d. Near Ocean City

6. What did Dicey recognize in the voice of the storekeeper in St. Michael's?
   a. That the clerk was a foreigner
   b. That the clerk sounded a little like her mother
   c. That the clerk was originally from Connecticut
   d. That the clerk was afraid of her

Multiple Choice Quizzes continued page 16

7. What did the children recognize in the looks of the young people on the Eastern Shore?
   a. Their own likeness
   b. People like the ones they had known in Provincetown
   c. People like Windy and Stewart from the college
   d. People from the circus

8. Who did the children meet at the circus in Easton?
   a. Edie and Louis
   b. Jerry and Tom
   c. Eunice and Joseph
   d. Claire and Will

Multiple Choice Quizzes continued page 17

Part II Chapters 5 & 6
1. What do the children decide to do to make some money?
    a. Sell subscriptions to magazines
    b. Sweep floors
    c. Become tomato pickers
    d. Join the circus

2. Why wouldn't Dicey agree to leave even when she felt uneasy about Mr. Rudyard?
    a. Because she had given her word to pick a lot of tomatoes
    b. Because she didn't trust her own instincts
    c. Because they hadn't been paid yet
    d. Because she wanted to stay in that town for a while

3. How did Mr. Rudyard keep the children in the field even after Dicey said they had to leave?
    a. He threatened to call the police.
    b. He threatened them with his dog.
    c. He said he wouldn't pay them.
    d. He said that by law the children had to stay another hour.

4. What diverted the dog's attention from tracking the children?
    a. Mrs. Rudyard's voice
    b. The leftover biscuits
    c. Some dog food in the pickup truck
    d. Another dog

5. How did the children escape from Mr. Rudyard?
    a. They hid in his barn.
    b. They bribed another picker to help them.
    c. They swam down the river.
    d. They hid in a tree.

6. How did Mr. Rudyard continue to pursue the Tillermans?
    a. By boat
    b. By bus
    c. In his pickup truck and on foot
    d. By swimming after them

Multiple Choice Quizzes continued page 18

7. Who saved the children from Mr. Rudyard?
    a. Louis and Edie
    b. The police
    c. Some passing motorists
    d. The people with the circus

8. What did Mr. Rudyard try to claim?
    a. That the Tillermans had stolen from him
    b. That the Tillermans were wanted by the law
    c. That he was their grandfather
    d. That the Tillermans were his foster children

9. Who personally ran Mr. Rudyard off?
    a. A police officer who shot at him
    b. Will
    c. Sampson
    d. Claire

Multiple Choice Quizzes continued page 19

Part II Chapter 7

1. How did the children get to Crisfield?
    a. Claire went with them on the bus.
    b. Will drove them there.
    c. They walked.
    d. They went on a boat.

2. What assurance did Will give the children before leaving them?
    a. That he would get them tickets to the next year's circus
    b. That they could always call on him for help
    c. That he would check back with them in a week
    d. That he was pretty sure their grandmother would want them

3. What did Dicey tell the woman in the Crisfield store about why she was looking for Abigail Tillerman?
    a. She said she was desperate for someone to help her.
    b. She said that Abigail Tillerman was a friend of her father's.
    c. She said that she wanted to work on the farm.
    d. She said that Abigail Tillerman was expecting her arrival.

4. What was the word that occurred to Dicey to describe her first view of her grandmother's farm?
    a. Neat
    b. Abandoned
    c. Forlorn
    d. Beautiful

5. Where did Dicey finally find her grandmother?
    a. Hiding behind the curtains in the living room
    b. In the barn
    c. Sitting out on the back steps
    d. Behind the house in the woods

6. What does Dicey quote when her grandmother asks what she thinks of death?
    a. An old hymn her mother had taught her
    b. What she had read earlier on the tombstone about being home from the hill and the sea
    c. A Biblical proverb
    d. Something her mother once said to her

Multiple Choice Quizzes continued page 20

7. Why does Dicey's grandmother say she is glad her husband died?
   a. Because he was mean
   b. Because she never loved him
   c. Because he always wanted her to polish his shoes instead of polishing them himself
   d. Because now she had the whole property to herself

Multiple Choice Quizzes continued page 21

Part II Chapter 8

1. How did her grandmother surprise Dicey just as Dicey was turning to leave?
    a. She said she knew who Dicey was and that Dicey couldn't stay there.
    b. She suddenly smiled and asked her to come inside.
    c. She said she knew where Dicey's mother had gone.
    d. She threatened her with a gun.

2. How did her grandmother know who Dicey was?
    a. She was very intuitive.
    b. She had been told by the people in town.
    c. She had received a letter from Cousin Eunice in Bridgeport.
    d. She had received notice from the police.

3. What does her grandmother finally offer the family?
    a. She gives them fifty dollars.
    b. She offers to let them sleep there for one night.
    c. She offered to talk to Cousin Eunice for them.
    d. She offered to call Will from the circus.

4. How did Dicey and her grandmother get back to Crisfield.
    a. Walking
    b. Traveling in her grandmother's boat
    c. Driving with a neighbor
    d. Taking the bus

5. What happened when Dicey returned to Crisfield for her three siblings?
    a. Only Sammy had waited there for her.
    b. Maybeth was missing.
    c. They refused to go back to the farm with her.
    d. Sammy was lost.

6. How did James and Maybeth get to the farm from town?
    a. The woman from the grocery store drove them.
    b. Will and Claire gave them a ride.
    c. They hitchhiked.
    d. They walked.

Multiple Choice Quizzes continued page 22

7. Why was Dicey upset with James?
    a. Because he only took Maybeth with him
    b. Because she had told him to wait for her with the younger children
    c. Because he had the only map
    d. Because he made her look bad in front of her grandmother

8. What surprising thing did Dicey find out in the barn?
    a. A dead body
    b. A sailboat
    c. An old car
    d. A whole litter of kittens

9. What decision does Dicey make about her grandmother's house?
    a. Dicey decides that the farm is the right place for her and her siblings.
    b. Dicey decides that the farm should be sold.
    c. Dicey decides that she would rather be with Cousin Eunice than to live there.
    d. Dicey decides that it would never be here home.

10. What did the Tillerman children first learn to eat at their grandmother's house?
    a. Mussels
    b. Crabs
    c. Spaghetti
    d. Pizza

Multiple Choice Quizzes continued page 23

Part II Chapters 9 & 10
1. What question about her grandmother did Dicey start trying to answer the first morning there?
   a. She wanted to know what her grandmother had looked like when young.
   b. She wanted to know what her grandmother was like inside, not just outside.
   c. She wanted to know how much money her grandmother had.
   d. She wanted to know if she could convince her that the Tillermans could stay.

2. What project did the children choose for their first day at their grandmother's house?
   a. Repairing the sailboat
   b. Canning
   c. Pulling down the honeysuckle vines
   d. Cleaning the inside of the house

3. What did the children's grandmother say her husband did with books?
   a. Read too many of them
   b. Used them to build a wall to keep things out
   c. Made other people feel inferior
   d. Used them to get into college

4. What presents did the children receive when Will and Claire visited the farm?
   a. Free circus tickets
   b. A kitten
   c. Bicycles
   d. New underwear

5. What did her grandmother respond when Dicey asked if she expected the children to stay?
   a. She asked for more time to think.
   b. She said no.
   c. She said yes.
   d. She just nodded.

Multiple Choice Quizzes continued page 24

Part II Chapters 11 & 12

1. What did Dicey and her grandmother talk about privately in the kitchen late at night?
    a. Recipes
    b. The past—her grandmother's and her mother's
    c. James
    d. The Eastern Shore

2. What had their grandmother decided by the next morning about the children's future?
    a. To let them stay until Cousin Eunice had responded to her letter
    b. To make them leave the next day
    c. To pay for their bus fare back to Bridgeport
    d. To keep them with her

3. What did the Tillermans and their grandmother do at the school the next morning?
    a. Made arrangements for their records to be transferred to Bridgeport
    b. Got the children registered for school in Crisfield
    c. Had Maybeth tested for retardation
    d. Told the principal that they would not be attending there right away

4. What was Maybeth's major accomplishment of the day?
    a. She cleaned crabs by herself.
    b. She counted to 100.
    c. She read aloud to her grandmother.
    d. She stayed by herself for testing and was good enough to get placed in third grade

5. How did the children's grandmother introduce them to the woman in the grocery store?
    a. As migrant workers
    b. As the children of a friend of hers
    c. As her grandchildren
    d. As her neighbor's children

6. What major concession does the children's grandmother make at the dock?
    a. That she really doesn't hate all children
    b. That the children can stay with her
    c. That she will phone Cousin Eunice
    d. That she will let the children pull all of the honeysuckle down

49

Multiple Choice Quizzes continued page 25

7. What special question did Dicey ask her grandmother?
    a. If she could fix dinner that night
    b. If she could fix the sailboat up and have it
    c. If Maybeth could have her own room
    d. If James could go away to school

8. What important question did the children's grandmother ask just before they left the dock?
    a. She asked if they could swim.
    b. She asked if they were hungry.
    c. She asked if they were ready to go home.
    d. She asked if they wanted crabs or mussels for supper.

Key: Multiple Choice Quizzes

BOOK PART I (by chapter groupings)

1 & 2	3 & 4	5 & 6	7 & 8	9	10 & 11	12
1C	1A	1D	1C	1B	1B	1A
2D	2A	2D	2B	2B	2B	2B
3C	3B	3A	3D	3B	3C	3B
4B	4D	4C	4D	4D	4D	4C
5C	5B	5B	5A	5B	5C	5B
6B	6D	6A	6B	6C	6B	6A
7B	7C	7A	7A	7A	7A	
8D	8B	8D	8A	8C	8A	
9A	9C	9C			9C	
10A	10B	10A				

BOOK PART II (by chapter groupings)

1 & 2	3 & 4	5 & 6	7	8	9 & 10	11 & 12
1C	1B	1C	1B	1A	1B	1B
2A	2C	2C	2B	2C	2C	2A
3D	3B	3B	3C	3B	3B	3B
4A	4D	4B	4B	4B	4C	4D
	5B	5C	5C	5A	5B	5C
	6B	6C	6B	6D		6B
	7A	7D	7C	7B		7B
	8D	8D		8B		8C
		9D		9A		
				10B		

VOCABULARY WORKSHEETS

Vocabulary
Homecoming

Book Part I <u>Chapters 1 and 2</u> Part I: Using Prior Knowledge and Contextual Clues
Below are the sentences in which the vocabulary words appear in the text. Read the sentence. Use any clues you can find in the sentence combined with your prior knowledge and write what you think the underlined words mean in the space provided.

1. She **gnawed** away at what was bothering her.

2. Dicey kept her feet on the dash, and her body **slouched** down.

3. After a few minutes, Dicey **hustled** them all out of the car and trailed after them as they entered the mall.

4. The mall was built like a fortress around a huge, two-story enclosed street, where store **succeeded** store, as far as you could see.

5. Outside, beyond the covered sidewalk that ran like a **moat** around the huge building, lay the huge, gray parking lot, a no-man's-land of empty cars.

6. …sitting as they were in a **cocoon** of darkness, she should feel safe.

7. "It runs in families. **Hereditary** craziness."

8. James **elaborated** the plan.

9. The **raucous** cars roared past, unheeding.

10. He was **naughty**, but not mean.

Part II: Determining the Meaning   Match the vocabulary words to their dictionary definitions.

__ 1.	gnawed	A.	mischievous
__ 2.	slouched	B.	wide ditch filled with water
__ 3.	welled	C.	rough sounding; harsh
__ 4.	succeeded	D.	came after
__ 5.	moat	E.	expressed in greater detail
__ 6.	cocoon	F.	drooped
__ 7.	hereditary	G.	rose up
__ 8.	elaborated	H.	comfortable retreat; refuge
__ 9.	raucous	I.	bit, chewed on
__ 10.	naughty	J.	genetically transmitted

Vocabulary continued page 2

Book Part I Chapters 3 and 4 Part I: Using Prior Knowledge and Contextual Clues
Below are the sentences in which the vocabulary words appear in the text. Read the sentence. Use any clues you can find in the sentence combined with your prior knowledge and write what you think the underlined words mean in the space provided.

1. The sun was rising over the trees behind the brook, rising in waves of **molten** pink.

2. He hurtled his little body at his brother, using his feet to kick as fast as his hands **pummeled**.

3. Sammy put his hand in hers and came **trudging** along.

4. Mama wore her yellow dress with the **flounces**, and she had flowers in her hair.

5. Once again they set off, walking four **abreast**.

6. Silence and **solitude**; she might have been alone in the world.

7. "All right," she cried, **exasperated**.

8. "But if I fall asleep within about half an hour, you better call an ambulance. The danger is lapsing into a **coma**.

Part II: Determining the Meaning   Match the vocabulary words to their dictionary definitions.

___ 11. molten   A.   deep prolonged unconsciousness
___ 12. pummeled   B.   walking laboriously
___ 13. trudging   C.   impatient
___ 14. flounces   D.   beat
___ 15. abreast   E.   state of being alone
___ 16. solitude   F.   made liquid and glowing
___ 17. exasperated   G.   gathered material attached to a skirt
___ 18. coma   H.   side by side

Vocabulary continued page 3

Book Part I <u>Chapters 5 and 6</u> Part I: Using Prior Knowledge and Contextual Clues
Below are the sentences in which the vocabulary words appear in the text. Read the sentence. Use any clues you can find in the sentence combined with your prior knowledge and write what you think the underlined words mean in the space provided.

1. A heron looked up at them, curious but not afraid, before he flew to a more **secluded** spot.

2. "It's **convalescent** food."

3. Louis said it was illegal to fish in the marsh, because that area was a game **sanctuary**.

4. …I was going to try to get work at the store by the park, but I was afraid we'd get too **conspicuous** when we had to stay….

5. The folds of the hills and the **symmetry** of the trees no longer had the power to please them.

6. Then the children **stealthily** approached the boat.

7. They pulled up beside a boat that was dark and empty and tied their **dinghy** to its stern.

8. The silence **vibrated**, as if with things beneath it struggling to break through.

Part II: Determining the Meaning Match the vocabulary words to their dictionary definitions.

___ 19. secluded	A.	shook; trembled
___ 20. convalescent	B.	balanced or harmonious proportions
___ 21. sanctuary	C.	set apart
___ 22. conspicuous	D.	secretly; furtively
___ 23. symmetry	E.	small open boat; rowboat
___ 24. stealthily	F.	for someone recuperating from illness or injury
___ 25. dinghy	G.	obvious
___ 26. vibrated	H.	place of refuge

Vocabulary continued page 4

Book Part I Chapters 7 and 8 Part I: Using Prior Knowledge and Contextual Clues
Below are the sentences in which the vocabulary words appear in the text. Read the sentence. Use any clues you can find in the sentence combined with your prior knowledge and write what you think the underlined words mean in the space provided.

1. Day by day, their money **dwindled** away.

2. Sometimes they would **glimpse** a face through an open window.

3. Rain showered down and made miniature puddles on the **turgid** river water.

4. She **revolved** slowly, her eyes closed, like a wind-up toy that was running down.

5. James' eyes were on the floor and his hands were **clenched** in his pockets.

6. Then he played a slow, **mournful** melody on it, concentrating hard, biting his lip, leaning over the instrment and moving his shoulders with the rhythm.

7. The children wandered up and down while Stewart and Dicey sat watching the little waves that **meandered** up onto the smooth sand.

8. She turned quickly to look at his face, but he was looking out over the water, his gray-blue eyes **glinting** in its reflections.

Part II: Determining the Meaning Match the vocabulary words to their dictionary definitions.

__ 27.	dwindled	A.	sparkling
__ 28.	glimpse	B.	became less
__ 29.	turgid	C.	causing or suggesting sadness
__ 30.	revolved	D.	moved aimlessly and idly
__ 31.	clenched	E.	see briefly
__ 32.	mournful	F.	closed tightly
__ 33.	meandered	G.	swollen
__ 34.	glinting	H.	turned; rotated

Vocabulary continued page 5

Book Part I <u>Chapter 9</u> Part I: Using Prior Knowledge and Contextual Clues
Below are the sentences in which the vocabulary words appear in the text. Read the sentence. Use any clues you can find in the sentence combined with your prior knowledge and write what you think the underlined words mean in the space provided.

1. "**Amnesia**," James suggested.

2. Her lips **pursed**.

3. "We are family, aren't we? And when I think of you, all alone—**abandoned**—like myself really, in a way…."

4. Dicey nodded, with her eyes on his, but she was **reciting** to herself: *Crisfield. Eastern Shore. Maryland.*

5. She was **lulled** to sleep by the words repeating in her head: *Crisfield, Eastern Shore, Maryland.*

Part II: Determining the Meaning Match the vocabulary words to their dictionary definitions.

___ 35. amnesia   A.   puckered
___ 36. pursed   B.   given up; left behind
___ 37. abandoned   C.   soothed
___ 38. reciting   D.   loss of memory
___ 39. lulled   E.   repeating

Vocabulary continued page 6

Book Part I Chapters 10 & 11 Part I: Using Prior Knowledge and Contextual Clues
Below are the sentences in which the vocabulary words appear in the text. Read the sentence. Use any clues you can find in the sentence combined with your prior knowledge and write what you think the underlined words mean in the space provided.

1. They nodded **solemnly** at her, then she pulled out her hand from behind her back and tossed the red ball to Sammy.

2. Other people's old clothes—Dicey **quelled** the thought.

3. "Your Cousin Eunice is a **devout** Catholic," he said.

4. The little girl **scowled** down at the cake.

5. "…Remember, this is **conjecture,** not fact.…"

6. "…James, fortunately, is **biddable**. Sammy has to be brought into line, so he doesn't shame me."

Part II: Determining the Meaning Match the vocabulary words to their dictionary definitions.

__ 40. solemnly   A.   obedient; docile
__ 41. quelled   B.   guesswork
__ 42. devout   C.   put down forcibly
__ 43. scowled   D.   somberly; earnestly
__ 44. conjecture   E.   frowned
__ 45. biddable   F.   deeply religious; sincere

Vocabulary continued page 7

Book Part I Chapter 12 Part I: Using Prior Knowledge and Contextual Clues
Below are the sentences in which the vocabulary words appear in the text. Read the sentence. Use any clues you can find in the sentence combined with your prior knowledge and write what you think the underlined words mean in the space provided.

1. The girls wore **organdy** dresses and party shoes and ribbons in their hair, or hats.

2. When Cousin Eunice called her, the women stepped back and smiled **primly** at her.

3. Dicey watched him catch a flying swing and leap onto it, then jump furiously with his **sturdy** little legs.

4. And then, Dicey thought to herself as the soft voice **droned** on about service and prayer, just when Cousin Eunice was about to do what she'd always wanted, the Tillermans turned up to tie her down again. Poor Cousin Eunice.

5. "I guess she's slow at school, but I don't think she's **retarded**. Or anything like that."

6. She was arguing more from habit than **conviction**.

7. "I thought so!" he **crowed**, laughing at her as she stood, open-mouthed, the suitcase in one hand, the door knob in the other. "You can't fool me!"

Part II: Determining the Meaning Match the vocabulary words to their dictionary definitions.

__ 46. organdy	A.	properly; precisely
__ 47. primly	B.	exulted loudly; boasted
__ 48. sturdy	C.	slow in development
__ 49. droned	D.	strong; healthy
__ 50. retarded	E.	stiff fabric of cotton or silk
__ 51. conviction	F.	spoke in a monotonous tone
__ 52. crowed	G.	strong belief or opinion

Vocabulary continued page 8

Book Part II Chapters 1 & 2 Part I: Using Prior Knowledge and Contextual Clues
Below are the sentences in which the vocabulary words appear in the text. Read the sentence. Use any clues you can find in the sentence combined with your prior knowledge and write what you think the underlined words mean in the space provided.

1. Maybeth smiled, a **tenuous** little smile, and turned back to the window.

2. The **circuitous** route from Baltimore to Annapolis, where they kept getting on and off the same road to stop at little huts by the road and let off passengers, took another hour and a half.

3. Across this circle, a quiet finger of water, hemmed in by concrete, marked the corner of a narrow area where people **thronged**, eating, talking, sitting and watching one another.

4. Great, heavy **arcs** of water shot out from the boat, spraying everywhere.

5. Sammy had lost interest in the conversation and was lying on his stomach on the deck, trying to **dabble** his hand in the water.

6. She picked up her bag from the dock and **hustled** everyone ahead of her down the dock.

7. They wandered around again until evening had settled in, milling with crowds of people who seemed to have nothing else to do but **saunter** down the streets and look in store windows, or peer at the little houses.

Part II: Determining the Meaning Match the vocabulary words to their dictionary definitions.

___ 53. tenuous   A. walk leisurely
___ 54. circuitous   B. crowded together
___ 55. thronged   C. hurried along
___ 56. arcs   D. slight
___ 57. dabble   E. splash
___ 58. hustled   F. roundabout
___ 59. saunter   G. shapes like curves

Vocabulary continued page 9

Book Part II Chapters 3 & 4 Part I: Using Prior Knowledge and Contextual Clues
Below are the sentences in which the vocabulary words appear in the text. Read the sentence. Use any clues you can find in the sentence combined with your prior knowledge and write what you think the underlined words mean in the space provided.

1. His hand sketched a **zigzag** motion in the air.

2. Because life wasn't really an ocean, and she wasn't really a little boat **bobbling** about on it.

3. "Most men lead lives of quiet **desperation**," Jerry said.

4. It wasn't power she felt, guiding the **tiller**, but purpose.

5. The boat **heeled** a little now, in the afternoon wind.

6. To make herself feel better, she **vowed** that she would sail again, and often, if she could.

Part II: Determining the Meaning Match the vocabulary words to their dictionary definitions.

  ___ 60. zigzag   A. tilted
  ___ 61. bobbling   B. despair
  ___ 62. desperation   C. lever that steers the boat
  ___ 63. tiller   D. promised solemnly; pledged
  ___ 64. heeled   E. moving about jerkily
  ___ 65. vowed   F. make sharp turns in alternating directions

Vocabulary continued page 10

Book Part II Chapters 5 & 6 Part I: Using Prior Knowledge and Contextual Clues
Below are the sentences in which the vocabulary words appear in the text. Read the sentence. Use any clues you can find in the sentence combined with your prior knowledge and write what you think the underlined words mean in the space provided.

1. Even from the road their **fatigue** was evident.

2. It charged against the fence, setting up a **clamor** that would rouse anyone in the house.

3. The ground **surged** up to meet her and the cab door slammed against her shoulder.

4. Pickers were scattered among tomato plants that rose up from the tops of **furrows**.

5. He was **intent** upon her face and her slow backing away.

6. A **cacophony** of noise burst out of the mass of tumbling dogs.

7. He hadn't entirely awakened Dicey from her **reverie**.

Part II: Determining the Meaning Match the vocabulary words to their dictionary definitions.

___ 66. fatigue   A.   jarring, discordant sound
___ 67. clamor   B.   state of musing; daydream
___ 68. surged   C.   loud outcry
___ 69. furrows   D.   moved up quickly; swelled
___ 70. intent   E.   weariness; exhaustion
___ 71. cacophony   F.   concentrated; firmly fixed
___ 72. reverie   G.   shallow trenches in the ground made by a plow

Vocabulary continued page 11

Book Part II Chapter 7 Part I: Using Prior Knowledge and Contextual Clues
Below are the sentences in which the vocabulary words appear in the text. Read the sentence. Use any clues you can find in the sentence combined with your prior knowledge and write what you think the underlined words mean in the space provided.

1. Most of the land was being used for farms, **interspersed** with loblollies and other trees.

2. "I got work to do," the woman continued, to **prod** Dicey.

3. The waves **gurgled** underneath them.

4. Often, their screens were ripped or doors hung **askew**.

5. The farmhouses sat next to the road, quiet and clean, **secretive**.

6. "The fact is you're **trespassing**," her grandmother said.

Part II: Determining the Meaning Match the vocabulary words to their dictionary definitions.

___ 73. interspersed   A.   made a kind of bubbling sound
___ 74. prod   B.   inclined to secrecy
___ 75. gurgled   C.   to one side; awry
___ 76. askew   D.   invading property or space of another
___ 77. secretive   E.   goad to action
___ 78. trespassing   F.   distributed randomly among

Vocabulary continued page 12

Book Part II <u>Chapter 8</u> Part I: Using Prior Knowledge and Contextual Clues
Below are the sentences in which the vocabulary words appear in the text. Read the sentence. Use any clues you can find in the sentence combined with your prior knowledge and write what you think the underlined words mean in the space provided.

1. "You're Liza's daughter. Some **ungodly** name she gave you, her and that Francis. I liked him, I did.

2. "Don't you lie to me, girl. If you didn't need a place to sleep you wouldn't have **traipsed** out here this morning. You wouldn't have come around back to find me...."

3. They glared at on e another across the kitchen. Neither one of them **faltered**.

4. Dicey scrambled out and **hoisted** herself up onto the boards.

5. "Because paper mulberries are **fragile**," her grandmother answered.

6. She went **abruptly** downstairs.

7. A fleeting expression that might have been unaccustomed **mirth**, or might have been a twinge of pain, went across her grandmother's face.

8. The woman didn't answer, but instead lifted up the basket and poured the **teeming** mass of crabs into the water.

Part II: Determining the Meaning Match the vocabulary words to their dictionary definitions.

___ 79. ungodly A. swarming
___ 80. traipsed B. weakened; became unsteady
___ 81. faltered C. walked
___ 82. hoisted D. suddenly; without warning
___ 83. fragile E. gladness
___ 84. abruptly F. outrageous
___ 85. mirth G. delicate; easily broken
___ 86. teeming H. raised; lifted

Vocabulary continued page 13

Book Part II <u>Chapters 9 & 10</u> Part I: Using Prior Knowledge and Contextual Clues
Below are the sentences in which the vocabulary words appear in the text. Read the sentence. Use any clues you can find in the sentence combined with your prior knowledge and write what you think the underlined words mean in the space provided.

1. Dicey woke herself up early the next morning before the first gray **signals** of dawn, when the air outside lay black over fields, marshes and the glistening water she could just see from her window.

2. If she wanted the Tillermans to go, then she wanted herself to go—in a **contradictory** way this was true.

3. "That honeysuckle's been there a long time. It's the kind of **tenacious** plant I have to respect," their grandmother said.

4. As they stood, patiently unraveling coiled **tendrils**, Dicey began to sing the song about the wide river and the small boat.

5. Her wet shorts **chafed** against her waist and thighs.

6. Her grandmother's fury burned behind her **immobile** face.

Part II: Determining the Meaning Match the vocabulary words to their dictionary definitions.

___ 87. signals   A.   unmoving; fixed
___ 88. contradictory   B.   rubbed
___ 89. tenacious   C.   signs
___ 90. tendrils   D.   asserting the opposite of
___ 91. chafed   E.   holding firm; stubborn
___ 92. immobile   F.   twisting, threadlike shoots of a plant

Vocabulary continued page 14

Book Part II Chapters 11 & 12 Part I: Using Prior Knowledge and Contextual Clues
Below are the sentences in which the vocabulary words appear in the text. Read the sentence. Use any clues you can find in the sentence combined with your prior knowledge and write what you think the underlined words mean in the space provided.

1. Her hair was all in **tousled** curls.

2. Her grandmother waved her hand, **vaguely**, to brush away the memories like you brush away cobwebs.

3. She liked her all prickly and **contrary**.

4. They saw flocks of gulls, gossiping, **bickering**, bobbling on the waves, flying in noisy swarms.

5. Her grandmother nodded her head **briskly**.

6. The abrupt change of topic **flustered** Millie.

7. Maybeth nodded and her eyes gleamed.

8. What was the use of **postponing** it?

Part II: Determining the Meaning Match the vocabulary words to their dictionary definitions.

__ 93. tousled	A.	squabbling; having little quarrels
__ 94. vaguely	B.	willful; perverse
__ 95. contrary	C.	rumpled; disheveled
__ 96. bickering	D.	glowed
__ 97. briskly	E.	lacking clear or distinct form
__ 98. flustered	F.	putting off until a later time
__ 99. gleamed	G.	made nervous or upset
__ 100. postponing	H.	in a quick, energetic way

Answer Key: Vocabulary
Homecoming

1.	I	26.	A	51.	G	76.	C
2.	F	27.	B	52.	B	77.	B
3.	G	28.	E	53.	D	78.	D
4.	D	29.	G	54.	F	79.	F
5.	B	30.	H	55.	B	80.	C
6.	H	31.	F	56.	G	81.	B
7.	J	32.	C	57.	E	82.	H
8.	E	33.	D	58.	C	83.	G
9.	C	34.	A	59.	A	84.	D
10.	A	35.	D	60.	F	85.	E
11.	F	36.	A	61.	E	86.	A
12.	D	37.	B	62.	B	87.	C
13.	B	38.	E	63.	C	88.	D
14.	G	39.	C	64.	A	89.	E
15.	H	40.	D	65.	D	90.	F
16.	E	41.	C	66.	E	91.	B
17.	C	42.	F	67.	C	92.	A
18.	A	43.	E	68.	C	93.	C
19.	C	44.	B	69.	G	94.	E
20.	F	45.	A	70.	F	95.	B
21.	H	46.	E	71.	A	96.	A
22.	G	47.	A	72.	B	97.	H
23.	B	48.	D	73.	F	98.	G
24.	D	49.	F	74.	E	99.	D
25.	E	50.	C	75.	A	100.	F

DAILY LESSONS

Lesson One

Objectives
1. To introduce the unit on **Homecoming**
2. To distribute books and other related materials (study guides, reading assignments, etc.)
3. To begin consideration and discussion of one theme in **Homecoming**, namely defining what "home" means to different people

NOTE: Prior to this lesson, students should have been instructed to think about what "home" means to them. One of the continuing themes in **Homecoming** is Dicey Tillerman's attempts to figure out what makes a home a home. Is it a person? Who must be in the home? Where must the home be? Is a home safety? Is it freedom? Is it always the same? Different people must answer these questions for themselves. You will have prepared ahead of time a bulletin board that has the title MY HOME: WHAT HOME MEANS TO ME. You may want to place pictures on the board. Remember to include pictures of both tangible and intangible things. For instance, you might have some pictures of things that people might have in their homes but will also want to show pictures of people embracing, people laughing together, people sleeping, people eating, etc. The point, of course, is that home can mean different things to different people.

Activity #1
Ask students individually to explain what home means to them. If they like, they can have prepared ahead of time a brief written description or they may just define home in a few sentences verbally. Whatever technique they choose is fine, as long as they demonstrate clearly some of the ways they would define "home." After they have explained their views, each student should go to the bulletin board and write one word that, for him or her, would follow the phrase, HOME IS…. But they may follow the phrase with only **one** word. A suggestion: Sometime near the end of the unit, if you have time, you may want to ask the students to repeat this assignment pretending that they are the Tillerman children. In fact, you might tell the students ahead of time to be thinking during the whole unit about which word each child—Dicey, James, Maybeth, and Sammy—would choose and why. This technique might help to tie the beginning and end of the unit together nicely and also serve to keep students focused on a main theme of the book.

Activity #2
Distribute the materials students will use in this unit. Explain in details how students are to use the materials.

Study Guides Students should read the study guide questions for each reading assignment before beginning the assignment to get a feeling for what events and ideas are important in the section they are about to read. After reading the section, students will (as a class or individually) answer the questions to review the important events and ideas from that section of the book. Students should keep the study guides as study materials for the unit test.

Lesson One continued page 2

Vocabulary As they are reading a section of the text, students will do vocabulary work related to the section they are reading. If they hunt for the vocabulary words as they read, students should be able to figure out the contextual meaning of the words. Following the completion of the reading of the book, there will be a vocabulary review of all the words used in the vocabulary assignments. Students should keep their vocabulary work as study materials for the unit test.

A special note: If you wish to make the vocabulary unit more challenging and perhaps more fun for your students, you might try having them use the words in sentences **not** relating to **Homecoming** and possibly trying to use all of the words in one section in a paragraph. These could be individual exercises or could be done on the blackboard as a class.

Reading Assignment Sheet You need to fill in the reading assignment sheet to let students know when their reading has to be completed. You can either write the assignment on a side black board or bulletin board and leave it there for students to see each day, or you can make copies for each student to have. In any case, advise students to become very familiar with the reading assignments so they know what is expected of them.

Extra Activities Center The unit resource portion of this unit contains suggestions for a library of related books and articles in your classroom as well as crossword and word search puzzles. Make a center in your room where you will keep these materials for students to use. (Bring the books and articles in from the library and keep several copies of the puzzles on hand.) Explain to students that these materials are available for their use when they finish reading assignments or other class work early.

Nonfiction Assignment Sheet Explain to students that they each are to read at least one nonfiction piece from the in-class library at some time during the unit. Students will fill out a nonfiction assignment sheet after completing the reading to help you evaluate their reading experiences and to help the students to think about and evaluate their own reading.

Books Each school has its own rules and regulations regarding student use of school books. Advise students of the procedures that are usual for your school.

NONFICTION ASSIGNMENT SHEET

(To be completed after reading the required nonfiction article)

Name _____ Date _____ Class _____

Title of Nonfiction Read _____

Author _____ Publication Date _____

I. **Factual Summary**: Write a short summary of the piece you read.

II. **Vocabulary**:
   1. Which vocabulary words were difficult?

   2. What did you do to help yourself understand the words?

III. **Interpretation**: What was the main point the author wanted you to get from reading his or her work?

IV. **Criticism**:
   1. Which points of the piece did you agree with or find easy to believe? Why?

   2. Which points did you disagree with or find hard to believe? Why?

V. **Personal Response**:
   1. What do you think about this piece?

   2. How does this piece help you better understand the novel, **Homecoming**?

Oral Reading Evaluation
Homecoming

Name _____ Class _____ Date _____

SKILL	EXCELLENT	GOOD	AVERAGE	FAIR	POOR
Fluency	5	4	3	2	1
Clarity	5	4	3	2	1
Audibility	5	4	3	2	1
Pronunciation	5	4	3	2	1
_____	5	4	3	2	1
_____	5	4	3	2	1

Total _____ Grade _____

Comments:

Lesson Two

Objectives
1. To preview with study questions, do the vocabulary on, and read Part I, 1 & 2.
2. To give students practice reading orally
3. To evaluate students' oral reading

Activity #1
Have students read Part I, 1 & 2 out loud in class. You probably know the best way to choose readers from your class: pick students at random, ask for volunteers, or use whatever other method works best for your group. If you have not yet completed an oral reading evaluation for your students this marking period, this would be a good opportunity to do so. A form is included with this unit for your convenience.

If students do not complete the reading assignment in class, they should do so prior to your next class meeting.

Lesson Three

Objectives
1. To preview with study questions, do the vocabulary on, and read Part I, 3 & 4
2. To focus students' attention on a discussion of the characters in the text

Activity #1
You may want to have students read aloud again, to give them practice in reading for the whole class. This method will have the added advantage of allowing you to see what reading levels your students are at and to further evaluate their abilities.

Activity #2
Even at this early point in **Homecoming**, readers can get a strong sense of the major characters—the Tillerman children. You might want to go around the room and allow students to assign one or two words to each of the children or simply to tell what their responses to the characters are at the end of four chapters. Because **Homecoming** is a rather long book, you want to make sure that students stay focused on repeated personality traits in order to end the book with a clear understanding of each character. Pointing students in this direction early will help to reinforce what you hope they will do throughout the book. Also, by hearing what other students think and why, students will think more deeply about the descriptions, themes, and events in the book.

Lesson Four

Objective

To explain the Nonfiction Reading Assignment to students and allow them time in the school library to get started on the assignment

Activity

Spend some time with the Nonfiction Reading Assignment Sheet (introduced earlier in this unit) and the topics and directions for the Nonfiction Reading Assignment that follow this lesson. Explain the assignment thoroughly to students, answer any questions that they may have, and then allow them to get underway on the assignment.

Notes to the teacher:

(1) There is nothing exhaustive or magical about my Nonfiction Reading Assignment list. If students have other ideas, their ideas may well be better choices for them. Also, if you would like to add to the list, by all means, do so. This is just a possible list to get you and your students started.

(2) You might want to alert the students to the fact that during the next class meeting you are going to ask them to tell one interesting fact that they have uncovered in their research for this assignment. Encourage students to be looking for something interesting that they think the rest of the class might like to know. Remind them that they are going to report one interesting fact, not give a report on their research. Giving this kind of very brief presentation will help students to discriminate items of particular interest from many different items and also to think clearly in terms of audience and how to choose information of interest to that audience.

Nonfiction Reading Assignment
Homecoming

For this assignment, you are to choose from the following list of topics some interesting aspect of the Chesapeake Bay area and research it. Be sure to choose something that is at least relatively interesting to you. If some topic not listed here appeals to you, you may talk with your teacher about researching it, but be sure that you have good reasons to justify why your topic is important and worth reading about.

If you and your teacher agree that it might be helpful, you may use the KWL form to get started on this assignment.

Possible Topics:
Maryland blue crabs
Picking crabs
Crabbing on the Bay
Chesapeake Bay Retriever dogs
Birds of the Eastern Shore
Eastern Shore industry
Eastern Shore recreation
Major attractions of Annapolis (or any town mentioned in **Homecoming**)
Oysters
Skipjacks
Preservation and care of the Bay
The Chesapeake Bay Bridge
Sailing
Fishing
Environmental issues
Picking vegetables
Modern movies set on the Eastern Shore
Farming

KWL
Homecoming

Directions: Before reading, think about what you already know about your assigned topic. Write the information in the K column. Think about what you would like to find out from reading the book. Write your questions in the W column. After you have read the book, use the L column to write the answers to your questions from the W column and anything else you remember from the book.

K WHAT I KNOW	W WHAT I WANT TO FIND OUT	L WHAT I LEARNED

Lesson Five

Objectives
1. To allow students to give brief responses regarding their Nonfiction Reading Assignment
2. To preview with study questions, do the vocabulary on, and read Part I, 5 & 6
3. To assign students to preview with study questions, do the vocabulary on, and read Part I, 7 & 8 at home in preparation for the next class.

Activity #1
Just go around the room and have each student tell his or her topic and then tell his or her interesting fact. It might be helpful to have students stand as they give their interesting fact, if only to focus their thinking and get them to take this brief presentation seriously. If you like, you may choose in the early going those students who will most likely have their facts totally prepared. But with fair warning, every student should be able to come up with one interesting thing to tell classmates. This activity will give you another opportunity to observe students as they present information to the class.

Activity #2
Spend some time during class doing the preview work for and reading Part I, 5 & 6.
Note to the teacher: If you like, you may add more critical questions to the fact-based short answer questions for class discussion. For example, for this class period, you could start with the fact-based questions and vocabulary. Then, if your students are prepared to move on, you might ask some questions about the section of reading, such as, What kind of person would be able to take over as head of the household at thirteen and lead her younger brothers and sisters across the country? Based on what you know already about Dicey's mother, what do you think she was thinking when she left her children in the mall parking lot? Do you think she loves her children? Think about the different people that the Tillermans are meeting. Whom would you rather go to for help? What is the difference between Sammy's swiping lunches and a wallet and Dicey's setting him up to go into the bakery and pretend to be something he is not? What kind of lessons do you think a six-year-old is learning on this journey to Bridgeport? Is there really a difference between Dicey's instructions to Sammy to be "sort of brave and pitiful" and Sammy's just walking up and taking a lunch that is lying around?

There are no doubt many other questions such as these that would provide a good foundation for class discussion, but these are a start. You will know best what your students are capable of and how much background work you might have to do to get them ready for critical discussions.

Activity #3
If you feel your students are capable of doing the preview, vocabulary, and reading work at home, assign chapters 7 & 8 for the next class.

Lesson Six

Objectives
1. To check the assigned work or to preview with study questions, do the vocabulary on, and read Part I, 7 & 8
2. To give students the opportunity to write from personal experience (Writing Assignment #1, Writing From Personal Experience)

Activity #1
Have students turn in the preview work if it was assigned for homework, or have students do the preview work in small groups or as a whole class during class time.

Activity #2
Give the students Writing Assignment #1 and allow them to write their papers during class time so that they have the opportunity to exchange papers with classmates prior to proofreading. If you run out of time, simply continue the writing assignment into the next class meeting.

Writing Assignment #1
(Writing from Personal Experience)

PROMPT

In the sections of the novel that you have read so far, you have learned a lot about the lives of the Tillerman children. You have gained an understanding of each child's personality, what makes each angry and what makes each smile, their value systems, their views in regard to their mother and to each other, and the relative strengths of each child. In eight chapters, then, the author of **Homecoming** has brought her main characters to life for you.

Your assignment is to choose one of two options:

One, you may write your assignment about yourself. Or, two, you may write your assignment about any of the four children in **Homecoming** and why you do or do not admire that character. If you choose the first option, you should be sure that at the end of your paper, your audience knows about at least three areas of your life. If you choose the second option, you should give at least three reasons for your decision.

Your choice should be relatively easy: if you find yourself especially interested in one of the characters, positively or negatively, then write about that character, or, if you are not particularly interested in any of the characters but would like to write about your own life, then write about yourself.

PREWRITING

For whichever choice you have made, make a list of the things that you would like to talk about. If you are writing about your own life, make a list of what you consider to be important areas in your life. If you are writing about one of the characters, make a list of what you consider to be favorable or unfavorable aspects of that character's life or traits that would make you do or do not admire.

Write down everything that occurs to you, and then go back and sort through them and combine ideas that are essentially the same. Pare your categories down until you have three basic points to make about yourself or about the character you have chosen. Then you can begin to write your paper.

DRAFTING

You will probably want to begin your paper with an interesting introductory paragraph in which you state your main point: I do/do not admire (your character). I lead an exciting life filled with interesting challenges. I lead a humdrum life filled with many boring experiences. Whatever you choose to say, state your point clearly in the first paragraph so that your audience knows what you are writing about.

Writing Assignment #1 continued page 2

Use your three main ideas for the body of the paper. Then write a conclusion that perhaps summarizes, looks to the future, or asks a question. Those are some of the ways that you can end your paper in a way that will be interesting to your audience.

PROMPT

When you finish the rough draft of your paper, ask a student who sits near you to read it. After reading your rough draft, he or she should tell you what he or she liked best about your work, which parts were difficult to understand, and ways in which your work could be improved. Reread your paper considering your critic's comments and make the corrections you think are necessary.

PROOFREADING

Do a final proofreading of your paper, double checking your grammar, spelling, organization, and the clarity of your ideas.

Lesson Seven

Objectives
1. To allow students to finish Writing Assignment #1 in class if time ran out in the preceding class
3. To test students' understanding of the first three sections of the novel
2. To preview with study questions, do the vocabulary on, and read Part I, 9

Activity #1
Give students as long as you deem is necessary for them to finish the first writing assignment during class time. Collect the assignment.

Activity #2
Use some of the questions from the Multiple Choice quizzes and test students' understanding of the first 8 chapters of Part I. After the quiz has been given, have students exchange papers and correct them right in the class. Collect the papers afterward, if you wish, but make sure that students have them to use for study purposes at the end of the unit.

Activity #3
Either as a whole class or in small groups, have students begin to preview Part I, chapter 9 with the study questions and the vocabulary worksheets. Then begin to read chapter 9 as a class. If you run out of time, you can simply ask students to finish the reading for chapter 9 at home.

Lesson Eight

Objectives
1. To preview with study questions, do the vocabulary on, and read Part I, 10 & 11
2. To allow students to get underway with the class project (Project Chesapeake Bay Country)

Activity #1
Spend some time during class doing the preview work for and reading Part I, 10 & 11.
Note to the teacher: If you like, you may add more critical questions to the fact-based short answer questions for class discussion. For example, for this class period, you could start with the fact-based questions and vocabulary. Then, if your students are prepared to move on, you might ask some questions about the section of reading, such as, Which person in Bridgeport is kindest to the Tillerman children? Cousin Eunice? Father Joseph? Sergeant Gordo? What would have happened if Aunt Cilla had still been alive? Do you think the children would have been happy in Bridgeport with her? What kind of person do you think Aunt Cilla was? How would you feel if Cousin Eunice were leaving you

Lesson Eight continued page 2

behind in her house with the kind of instructions she left? Do you feel that Dicey is an ungrateful person?

There are no doubt many other questions such as these that would provide a good foundation for class discussion, but these are a start. You will know best what your students are capable of and how much background work you might have to do to get them ready for critical discussions.

Activity #2
Give students time to get started on the class project if you are doing it. If not, you might give a multiple choice quiz or spend some additional time on critical questions.

Class Project
Project Chesapeake Bay Country

Objectives

Through their reading of **Homecoming**, students should become at least a little bit intrigued by the area around the Chesapeake Bay of Maryland. If you teach in some regions of the country, students may already be knowledgeable about some of the aspects of Chesapeake Bay country. You may in fact live very near or in that area. In other regions, students learn a great deal from what could be their first exposure to this part of the country.

In any event, this project will give students the opportunity to discover the educational components of their research, to relate their research to real life, and to find a way to better publicize the object of their research and/or to take steps to improve a situation that they have investigated and found to be in need of improvement.

Students will be extracting from their Nonfiction Reading Assignment research an aspect of Chesapeake Bay Country that would benefit from some sort of educational methods. It may be that courses need to be offered on a subject at a local college or community center. It may be that information needs to be communicated to people outside the community via advertising of some sort. The people in the community may benefit from information that can be conveyed in newspaper articles, television news reports, advertising, or letters to the editor. Perhaps some sort of articles could be written for magazines or newspapers explaining some aspects of the area that would be of interest to people in other areas of the country. Perhaps information needs to be conveyed to young people in the area about how to get started in some kind of employment or how to find a job in the area for the summer.

Whatever the situation, students should be able to explain the educational need in a sentence or two and then proceed with the activities of the project.

THE PROJECT

This project is separate from the rest of the unit on **Homecoming**, so you can either use it while you are reading and reviewing the play or as a separate mini-unit after you have completed the unit test for **Homecoming**. Also, having it as a separate project enables you to either eliminate it or to use it, without disturbing the flow of the unit as a whole.

Activity #1

Explain the assignment fully to students. Set whatever time limits you wish to set for the project. If you do the project, I encourage you to allow some time(s) later in the unit for students to do updates on the work they are doing.

Project continued page 2

Activity #2
Try to find someone knowledgeable in your area who can interact with your class. This might be someone in your community who has frequently traveled to or perhaps lived in the Chesapeake Bay area. In certain areas of the country, it might be a crabber or an oysterman who would be willing to speak with students in the classroom. It might be a local waterman who would be willing to have students visit him on the waterfront one day. It could be someone who writes about waterfront areas for the local newspaper. Or, if you are nowhere near a waterfront, you might get someone to come and talk about crop picking, modern bridges, religious views, or the rights of children.

And if you are unable to get someone to interact personally with your class, try at least to contact someone who is willing to respond to student letters or perhaps to make a tape about his or her work that the class can listen to. You might even want to correspond with someone who lives and works in the Chesapeake Bay area to get some views that can be shared with your class. Maybe an older person in Crisfield, Maryland, would be willing to write to students about old and new Crisfield. Or if you find yourself in a pinch, you might have students write to the Annapolis, Maryland Chamber of Commerce and secure information about an area like that. The point is not to find the perfect connection but to find a way of making the Chesapeake Bay area connect to your students' real lives.

Set up some kind of dialogue with the person or persons you choose. You might want to have students write questions and send them to the person. If you have found someone who will talk directly with the students, you can use the questions for the day that the person comes to class. If you like, you may have students write the letters inviting people to interact with the class, although you probably will save a lot of time by undertaking this responsibility yourself. And don't forget the internet. If your students have access to computers, they could actually request a lot of information over the internet.

Activity #3
Have students choose one aspect of their Nonfiction Reading Assignment research that particularly interests them and that lends itself to educational publicity and/or improvement. It might be helpful to you to spend some time meeting very briefly with students before they get started on their project, just so that you are assured that they have chosen a workable topic. Students should be able to state their topic, tell in a sentence or two how they think education would benefit the situation they are working on, and then lay out at least two major ways in which they will work to apply educational means to their subject.

Activity #4
Have students actually get underway in applying their educational ideas. You may allow class time for one or two days for this purpose or you may have the students do this work as homework.

Project continued page 3

Note to the teacher: Whatever educational steps students are going to take should actually be planned out. For example, if students think that a class should be offered at the local college, they should write up a course description, perhaps make up a mock syllabus, and include one or two items for the reading list. If they think that a letter writing campaign would be an educational benefit, then they should actually write some of the letters. If they think that an advertising campaign would be most beneficial, then they should actually design the advertising campaign. And so on.

One specific example may suffice. When I was living in Maryland myself, I acquired a Chesapeake Bay Retriever puppy. Despite the fact that the Chessie is the Maryland State Dog, almost no one I met seemed to know that piece of information. Here is a dog that has its origins solidly on the Eastern Shore of Maryland, yet few people in Maryland even know that they exist. I often thought it would be fun to present those dogs in some way to the people of Maryland. Maybe an article in some local newspapers. Perhaps a few television shots. Maybe just a letter to the editor to extol the qualities of the Chessie. Getting information out about the dogs would have been educational and could have improved the public's understanding of this breed.

Again, the idea is not to find the perfect subject to work on but instead to help students to find ways of connecting the literature they are reading to real life.

Lesson Nine

Objectives
1.	To do the preview and vocabulary work for and to read Part I, 12
2.	To give students the opportunity to write to persuade (Writing Assignment #1 - Writing To Persuade)

Activity #1
Spend some time during class doing the preview work for and reading Part I, 12.
Note to the teacher: If you like, you may add more critical questions to the fact-based short answer questions for class discussion. For example, for this class period, you could start with the fact-based questions and vocabulary. Then, if your students are prepared to move on, you might ask some questions about the section of reading, such as, What view of Catholicism is put forward in **Homecoming**? Is it a fair view? An accurate one? Do you think that Cousin Eunice would make a good nun? What do you think her relationship was with her mother, Aunt Cilla? How do you think the two women related to one another? If you were living at Cousin Eunice's house, would you behave as Dicey does? Do you think that Dicey is grateful enough to Counsin Eunice? When Cousin Eunice tells Dicey that she is giving up the sisterhood, she says, "You are my family now." How does Cousin Eunice's view of "family" compare to Dicey's?

These are just some critical possibilities that you might want to include in your classroom discussions. You will be the best judge of your students' abilities to make discussions of this sort most profitable.

Activity #2
Give the students Writing Assignment #1 and allow them to write their papers during class time so that they have the opportunity to exchange papers with classmates prior to proofreading. If you run out of time, simply continue the writing assignment into the next class meeting.

Writing Assignment #2
(Writing to Persuade)

PROMPT

In Part I of the novel, you have read of the travels and troubles of the Tillerman family. You also know that Dicey and the children are leaving Bridgeport to find the grandmother they have never met. But what if you were in Bridgeport with the children? Suppose you were asked for your opinion of whether they should stay or go? Based on the part of the novel that you have read so far, what would you advise Dicey to do? Their choices are (1) to return to Provincetown and try to find a way to live there, (2) to stay in Bridgeport either together with Cousin Eunice or separated into different homes, or (3) to leave and take their chances on finding and being able to get along with a grandmother who has already been described only in negative ways.

Your assignment is to choose one of three options: return, stay, or move on.

Your paper is meant to be as persuasively convincing as possible, so pick the option you feel most strongly about.

PREWRITING

For whichever choice you have made, make a list of your reasons for choosing it. If you think that Dicey should try to get her family back to Provincetown, then think of ways to say so forcefully and defend your point of view. If you think that the children can be cared for and happy in Bridgeport, examine ways to state that point of view and support it thoroughly. If you are suggesting that the Tillermans are right to move on, then choose specific reasons why you believe that position is valid.

Write down everything that occurs to you, and then go back and sort through them and combine ideas that are essentially the same. Pare your categories down until you have three basic reasons for your decision. Then you can begin to write your paper.

DRAFTING

You will probably want to begin your paper with an interesting introductory paragraph in which you state your main point: The Tillermans should give Cousin Eunice and Bridgeport another chance. Whatever you choose to say, state your point clearly in the first paragraph so that your audience knows what you are writing about.

Use your three main ideas for the body of the paper. Then write a conclusion that perhaps summarizes, looks to the future, or asks a question. Those are some of the ways that you can end your paper in a way that will be interesting to your audience.

Writing Assignment #2 continued page 2

PROMPT
When you finish the rough draft of your paper, ask a student who sits near you to read it. After reading your rough draft, he or she should tell you what he or she liked best about your work, which parts were difficult to understand, and ways in which your work could be improved. Reread your paper considering your critic's comments and make the corrections you think are necessary.

PROOFREADING
Do a final proofreading of your paper, double checking your grammar, spelling, organization, and the clarity of your ideas.

Lesson Ten

Objective
To give students an opportunity to understand the characters in **Homecoming** better by envisioning them in different contexts

Activity
This might prove an interesting and fun way to end Part I of **Homecoming.** Try to put aside one entire class to achieve this objective. What you are going to do is ask some of your students to do some role playing in front of the rest of the class. Because not everyone will have the opportunity to play a role in class, the other students will learn from observing. Both actors and observers should be encouraged to think about how the characters are going to act in each scenario. You will be the best judge of which students can be relied on to carry out the assignment with a reasonable degree of understanding and comfort.

Don't worry that you don't have enough time to accommodate this kind of role playing. Its object is not to rehearse or spend a lot of time preparing for the role playing. It is, instead, to think through very quickly how characters will act based on what students already know about them.

This activity will work best if you try to prepare the students to have a good time doing it. Make sure they realize that there is no totally right or totally wrong way to do the activity. Instead, they should listen closely to the scenarios that you lay out, think very quickly about how their assigned character would react to each, and then pretend to *be* that character to the best of their ability.

Choose the scenarios that you think your students will best understand. You may do one or two scenarios or all five. If you want, you can even make up new scenarios, with or without your students' help. Again, there is no right or wrong here. You are just moving the characters around a little bit in order to let students look at them a little differently and understand them a little bit better.

Read the scenario. Give students three to five minutes to prepare, and then give them five minutes to act out the scenario. The ONLY requirement is that students try as hard as possible to keep the character as he or she behaved in the book.

Scenario #1 Two students needed: Cousin Eunice Logan and the children's mother
Instead of the children's mother being confined to a mental hospital, pretend that she has been found back in Provincetown. Cousin Eunice travels to Provincetown to tell Liza that she should take back and care for her children. Liza is determined that the children should stay with Cousin Eunice. **Have Cousin Eunice share her thoughts with Liza and then have Liza respond accordingly**

Lesson Ten continued page 2

Scenario #2: Two students needed: Dicey and her father
Although Dicey hasn't seen her father since she was just a little girl, pretend that he returns to the family. Have him come to Cousin Eunice's house, for example, and allow him to explain what he thinks should be done with the children. Remember Dicey's earlier feelings for her father. ***Have Dicey's father state his views and then just let the conversation between the two take its course.***

Scenario #3: Two students needed: Father Joseph and James Tillerman
James has discovered that Dicey plans to go to Crisfield by herself. Not sure what to do, he goes to Father Joseph and explains what he knows. James feels torn between his family and his new educational opportunities. ***Have James share his contradictory feelings honestly with Father Joseph and have Father Joseph respond appropriately whenever it seems appropriate to do so.***

Scenario #4: Four students needed: Edie, Louis, Dicey, and James
Assume that Dicey has figured out how to contact Edie and Louis and wants their advice. Somehow they get together, and Dicey tells them about life with Cousin Eunice. Although still wary of them, Dicey thinks that they might be able to help her to plan what to do. The four of them meet and talk about possibilities. ***Have Dicey start the conversation and allow the others to enter into it whenever it seems appropriate.***

Scenario #5: Two students needed: Dicey and her mother
Suppose for a moment that Dicey's mother had been at Cousin Eunice's house when the children arrived. What might she have said to Dicey and how might Dicey have responded? The mother may have a future plan or no plan at all. That is up to you. It is also up to you to decide whether Dicey's mother is currently mentally competent or not. ***Have Dicey's mother and Dicey share a conversation about what has already happened and what ought to happen now.***

Lesson Eleven

Objectives
1. To review Part I of the book
2. To test the students' understanding of Part I of the book.
3. To preview with study questions, do the vocabulary on, and read Part II, 1 & 2

Activity #1
Spend at least a few minutes making sure that students have understood Part I of the book. Touch briefly on the main events, characters, and themes in the first part.

Lesson Eleven continued page 2

Activity #2
Use some of the questions from the Multiple Choice quizzes and test students' understanding of the of Part I (or at least chapters 10-12) After the quiz has been given, have students exchange papers and correct them right in the class. Collect the papers afterward, if you wish, but make sure that students have them to use for study purposes at the end of the unit.

Activity #3
Spend some time during class doing the preview work for and reading Part II, 1 & 2.
Note to the teacher: If you like, you may add more critical questions to the fact-based short answer questions for class discussion. For example, for this class period, you could start with the fact-based questions and vocabulary. Then, if your students are prepared to move on, you might ask some questions about the section of reading, such as, What does Dicey mean when she thinks about settling for a place to stay free? What is the effect on the reader of having so many characters in the book think that Dicey is a boy? Who is the more admirable person, Jerry or Tom? Which would you most like to be friends with? What do you think Jerry and Tom's parents are really like?

As always, there are many other questions such as these that would provide a good foundation for class discussion, but these are a start. You will know best what your students are capable of and how much background work you might have to do to get them ready for critical discussions.

Lesson 12

Objectives
1. To preview with study questions, do the vocabulary on, and read Part II, 3 & 4
2. To give students an opportunity to update the class on their class projects, if you are doing that part of the unit, or
3. To give students the opportunity to think more about the themes and/or characters in **Homecoming**

Activity #1
Spend some time during class doing the preview work for and reading Part II, 2 & 3.
Note to the teacher: If you like, you may add more critical questions to the fact-based short answer questions for class discussion. For example, for this class period, you could start with the fact-based questions and vocabulary. Then, if your students are prepared to move on, you might ask some questions about the section of reading, such as, What is the effect of the Tillermans' trip going to be long-term on someone as young as Sammy? What values is he going to take away from their journey? Do students' views of Jerry and Tom change between chapter 2 and chapter three? What is the effect on the reader of the songs that the Tillerman children sing throughout the book? Why do you suppose the author included those scenes? What is the effect of Dicey's realizing that the young people

Lesson Twelve continued page 2

they were seeing looked a lot like them? What is the effect of Dicey's realizing that the store clerk sounded a little like her mother?

As always, there are many other questions such as these that would provide a good foundation for class discussion, but these are a start. You will know best what your students are capable of and how much background work you might have to do to get them ready for critical discussions.

Activity #2
If you are doing the class project, spend a part of this class allowing students to update the rest of the class on their progress.

Activity #3
If you want instead to talk about themes in the book, go around the room and ask each student to name a theme. There are enough to keep you going through most of the class: family ties, loyalty, courage, friendship, friendliness, values, love, compassion, understanding, children's rights, "smartness" or lack thereof, disabled children, determination, "craziness," searching for a home, religion, empathy, sympathy and concern versus pity, honesty versus dishonesty, search for roots, etc. One fun thing to do might be to have one student mention a theme and then another student supply an example of that theme. Just move from student to student until you think you have exhausted the subject. If you need additional ideas to fill in, do the same thing with characters. Have one student name a character and have the next student supply a word describing that person.

Lesson Thirteen

Objectives
1. To preview with study questions, do the vocabulary on, and read Part II, 5 & 6
2. To give students the opportunity to write to inform (Writing Assignment #3 - Writing To Inform)

Activity #1
Spend some time previewing the study questions and doing the vocabulary. Then either have students read silently at their desks or read aloud to the rest of the class.

Activity #2
Give the students Writing Assignment #3 and allow them to write their papers during class time so that they have the opportunity to exchange papers with classmates prior to proofreading.

Writing Assignment #3
(Writing to Inform)

PROMPT

In **Homecoming**, Dicey is an expert at reading maps. One of the first things we learn about her is that she has been awake since three in the morning reading maps and trying to find toll-free roads while her mother drove. Later we learn about a great many difficult things that Dicey can do. For example, she seems to know instinctively how to bargain for a job, how to make do with almost no funds and no food, how to deal with difficult people like Cousin Eunice and, later, her grandmother, how to control the younger children in her family, etc.

Your assignment is to choose something that you do well and can explain fully. Don't panic if you think you have nothing especially interesting to write on. The thing that you choose need not be extraordinary. For example, you may be able to play a particular sport, perform on a musical instrument, or sing in your church choir. On the other hand, you could just as well choose something seemingly more mundane, such as setting the table for dinner, getting a younger brother or sister dressed to go out, babysitting a child or children, getting the house ready for company, cleaning your own room, convincing one or both of your parents to allow you to do something, or even getting from your house to school each morning.

Choose an activity that you would like to write about and then think about who would like to know the information. The person or people who would like to know the information is your audience.

PREWRITING

A good way to start is to think through the activity thoroughly. Make a list of the things involved in the activity. Don't leave out important steps just because they are obvious to you. If you are informing someone how to get from their house to yours, for example, it would not do to leave out a major right hand turn onto a specific street just because you are used to making the turn.

Then try to group the items on your list by type. If you can group them into three categories, you will be well on your way to being able to write a clear, thorough paper.

DRAFTING

Begin your paper with an introductory paragraph. Your first paragraph might contain, for example, the reason for your writing in the first place. Then use one paragraph in the body of the paper for each of your three categories. And, finally, write a concluding paragraph that sums up your previous points, asks a question, offers the possibility of further information if the reader wants it, or broadens the subject out just a bit to include additional uses for the information.

Writing Assignment #3 continued page 2

PROMPT
When you finish the rough draft of your paper, ask a student who sits near you to read it. After reading your rough draft, he or she should tell you what he or she liked best about your work, which parts were difficult to understand, and ways in which your work could be improved. Reread your paper considering your critic's comments and make the corrections you think are necessary.

PROOFREADING
Do a final proofreading of your paper, double checking your grammar, spelling, organization, and the clarity of your ideas.

Lesson Fourteen

Objectives
1.   To complete the writing assignment from the previous class
2.   To preview with study questions, do the vocabulary on, and to read Part II, 7.

Activity #1
If students didn't finish the third writing assignment, you might like to give them part of the class period to finish it.

Activity #2
Spend some time discussing the study questions and doing the vocabulary for chapter 7, then read the chapter as a class.

Lesson Fifteen

Objectives
1.   To test students' understanding of the novel for Part II, 1-7
2.   To preview with study questions, do the vocabulary on, and read Part II, 8

Activity #1
Use some of the multiple choice quiz questions to test students' knowledge of the chapters read so far in Part II of the book. After the quiz has been given, have students exchange papers and correct them right in the class. Collect the papers afterward, if you wish, but make sure that students have them to use for study purposes at the end of the unit.

Activity #2
Spend some time discussing the study questions and the vocabulary for chapter 8.
Note to the teacher: If you like, you may add more critical questions to the fact-based short answer questions for class discussion. For example, for this class period, you could start with the fact-based questions and vocabulary. Then, if your students are prepared to move on, you might ask some questions about the section of reading, such as, What does James mean when he says that the Tillerman grandmother is "crazy like a fox"? Do you agree with his assessment? Why do you think the grandmother sat out on the back steps rather than hiding inside? What do you think the grandmother thought when she received the letter from Cousin Eunice? Why do you think Cousin Eunice wrote to the grandmother in the first place? Why was Dicey so joyful when she found the sailboat in the barn?

These are just some critical possibilities that you might want to include in your classroom discussions. You will be the best judge of your students' abilities to make discussions of this sort most profitable.

Lesson Sixteen

Objectives
1. To preview with study questions, do the vocabulary on, and read Part II, 9-10
2. To examine the characters in **Homecoming**

Activity #1
Spend some time discussing the study questions and the vocabulary for chapters 9-10, then read those chapters in class.

Activity #2
Take time to go around the room and let each student tell his or her most interesting character so far in the book. As each student names a character, he or she should be prepared to tell why they chose that character.

Lesson Seventeen

Objectives
1. To test students' knowledge of the whole novel, especially Sections 13 and 14
2. To review the main ideas and events of the whole novel

Activity #1
Choose some questions from the Multiple Choice Quizzes to test students' knowledge of the novel. You may choose only questions from Sections 13 and 14, or you may combine a series of multiple choice quiz questions from all of the choices offered.

Activity #2
Spend some time making sure that students understand the main ideas and events of the whole novel. Answer any questions that students still have about the book.

Lesson Eighteen

Objectives
1.   To preview with study questions and do the vocabulary on and then read Part II, chapters 11 & 12
2.   To do a brief review of the novel with the students

Activity #1
Spend time discussing the study questions and doing the vocabulary, then finish reading the book. Students may either read silently at their desks or aloud to the whole class.

Lesson Eighteen continued page 2

Activity #2
Do a brief review of the whole novel with students, just to make sure that they understand it as thoroughly as possible.

Lesson Nineteen

Objectives
1.   To have students exercise their critical thinking skills
2.   To try to relate some of the ideas in **Homecoming** to the students' lives

Activity #1
Choose the questions from the Extra Discussion Questions/Writing Assignments that seem most appropriate for your students. A class discussion of these questions is most effective if students have been given the opportunity to formulate answers to the questions prior to the discussion. To this end, you may either have all the students formulate answers to all of the questions, divide your class into groups and assign one or more questions to each group, or assign one question to each student in your class. The option you choose will obviously make a difference in the amount of class time needed for this activity.

Activity #2
After students have had ample time to formulate answers to the questions, begin your class discussion of the questions and the ideas presented by the questions. Be sure students take notes during the discussion so they have information to study for the unit test.

Activity #4
Try to spend some time on the critical/personal response and personal response questions in order to give the students ways to think personally about the play's events, main ideas, and characters.

Extra Discussion Questions/Writing Assignments
Homecoming

Interpretive
1. **Homecoming** is told from the third person point of view, that is, the narrator talking about Dicey and her family. How would the book change if Dicey herself were telling the story? What if James, Sammy, or Maybeth told the story?

2. What are the major obstacles that Dicey and her siblings have to overcome? What are the most important three obstacles?

3. Did you ever wonder if Dicey and her family would get to a safe home? If not, how did the author show you ahead of time that she would get home in the end? Were their clues along the way?

4. Explain the background and personality of Abigail Tillerman, the children's grandmother.

5. What, if any, do you suppose is the significance of Dicey's family name, Tillerman?

6. Is Homecoming the best title for the book? If so, why. If not, what would you suggest it be called instead?

7. Is the journey of the Tillerman children believable?

Critical
9. Are the characters in the story realistic? Explain.

10. How is repetition used in the novel? What is the purpose of repeating certain descriptions and phrases? Give specific examples to explain your thoughts.

11. Do the Tillerman children grow during the book, or are they about the same at the end as they were at the beginning? Explain your answer.

12. What do you think Cynthia Voigt's feelings are about children?

13. Name three themes in **Homecoming** and give an example of how each is developed.

14. In light of the whole novel, how do you explain the inscription on the tombstone that Dicey saw: *Home is the hunger, home from the hill, and the sailor home from the sea*?

15. What does the open water symbolize for Dicey?

Extra Discussion Questions continued page 2

Critical/Personal

16. Who is the most individualistic person in the novel? Support your belief.

17. Which person in the book is the most harmful to others? Support your belief.

18. Who in the book does the most good for others? Support your belief.

19. If you were Dicey, do you think you would have made the decisions that she did? Explain our answer.

Personal Response

20. Did you like **Homecoming**? Would you recommend it to other students?

21. Do you agree with Dicey that keeping a family together is of paramount importance? Explain your point of view.

22. Would you like Abigail Tillerman to be your grandmother? Why or why not?

23. Of all the places that the Tillerman children visit, where would you most like to go? Explain.

24. Do you know anyone like any of the characters in **Homecoming**. If so, who? Explain if you are comfortable doing so.

Quotations

25. It runs in families. Hereditary craziness."

26. "…He'd call me his little only. I don't know why."

27. "We are family, aren't we? And when I think of you, all alone—abandoned—like myself really, in a way….."

28. "…It will be hard to place Maybeth. A retarded child—"

29. "I had a dream that you were all on a bus and the door closed and I couldn't get on. I ran and ran after it, but it kept getting away."

30. "It was eating the biscuits!" she cried. "He couldn't get it to chase us because it was hungry. Doesn't that serve him right."

Extra Discussion Questions continued page 3

31. "And I've been chased by dogs myself often enough not to be overly scared of them. Animal dogs or human dogs."

32. "You're a little bit of my life now. You can't get away, and I can't get rid of you. That's a fact."

33. "Crazy as a coot, that's my opinion. We leave her alone. You should too."

34. "I know who you are. You hear me. I know who you are, and you can't stay here."

Lesson Twenty

Objective
To complete discussions begun in Lesson Nineteen

Activity
Since part of Lesson Nineteen was taken up with giving students time to formulate answers, you will probably need a substantial portion of this class period to complete your class discussions. Note to the teacher: If your discussions finish early or if you choose not to continue them into this class, you could give students this class period to review their own class notes, to give another brief report on the class project, to give a quick multiple choice quiz, or to do the alternate bulletin board activity mentioned in the first lesson.

Lesson Twenty-one

Objective
To review all of the vocabulary work done in this unit.

Activity
Choose one (or more) of the vocabulary review activities listed on the following pages and spend your class period as directed in the activity. Some of the materials for these review activities are located in the Extra Activities Packet in this unit.

Vocabulary Review Activities

1. Divide your class into two teams and have an old-fashioned spelling or definition bee.

2. Give each of your students (or students in groups of two, three, or four) a Vocabulary Word Search Puzzle based on **Homecoming**. The person or group to find all of the vocabulary words in the puzzle first wins.

3. Give students a **Homecoming** Vocabulary Word Search Puzzle without the word list. The person or group to find the most vocabulary words in the puzzle wins.

4. Use a **Homecoming** Vocabulary Crossword Puzzle. Put a puzzle onto a transparency on the overhead projector so everyone can see it and do the puzzle together as a class.

5. Give students a **Homecoming** Vocabulary Matching Worksheet to do.

Lessen Twenty-one continued page 2

6. Divide your class into two teams. Use the **Homecoming** vocabulary words with their letters jumbled as a word list. Student 1 from Team A faces off against Student 1 from Team B. You write the first jumbled word on the board. The first student (1A or 1B) to unscramble the word wins the chance for his or her team to score points. If 1A wins the jumble, go to student 2A and give him or her a definition. He or she must give you the correct spelling of the vocabulary word which fits that definition. If he or she does, Team A scores a point, and you give student 3A a definition for which you expect a correctly spelled matching vocabulary word. Continue giving Team A definitions until some team member makes an incorrect response. An incorrect response sends the game back to the jumbled-word face-off, this time with students 2A and 2B. Instead of repeating giving definitions to the first few students of each team, continue with the student after the one who gave the last incorrect response on the team. For example, if Team B wins the jumbled-word face-off and student 5B gave the last incorrect answer for Team B, you would start this round of definition questions with student 5B and so on. The team with the most points wins!

7. Have students write a story in which they correctly use as many vocabulary words as possible. Have students read their compositions orally! Post the most original compositions on your bulletin board.

Lesson Twenty-two

<u>Objective</u>
To review the main ideas presented in **Homecoming** using the extra activities in the unit plan

<u>Activity #1</u>
Choose one of the review games/activities included in the Extra Activities Packet and spend your class period as outlined there.

<u>Activity #2</u>
Remind students that the Unit Test will be given during the next class meeting. Stress the review of the Study Guides and their class notes as a last-minute, brush-up review for homework.

Review Games/Activities - Homecoming

1. Ask the class to make up a unit test for **Homecoming**. The test should have four sections: matching, short answer, multiple choice, and essay. Students may use half the period to make the test and then swap papers and use the other half of the class period to take a test a classmate has devised. The test should be taken open book. You may want to use the unit test included in this packet or take questions from the students' unit tests to formulate your own test.

2. Take half the period for students to make up short answer questions. Collect the questions. Divide the class into two teams. Alternate asking questions to individual members of teams A & B (like in a spelling bee). The question keeps going from A to B until it is correctly answered, then a new question is asked. A correct answer does not allow the team to get another question. Correct answers are +2 points; incorrect answers are -1 point.

3. Have students pair up and quiz each other from their study guides and class notes.

4. Give students a **Homecoming** crossword puzzle to complete.

5. Divide your class into two teams. Use the **Homecoming** crossword words with their letters jumbled as a word list. Student 1 from Team A faces off against Student 1 from Team B. You write the first jumbled word on the board. The first student (1A or 1B) to unscramble the word wins the chance for his or her team to score points. If 1A wins the jumble, go to student 2A and give him or her a clue. He or she must give you the correct word which matches that clue. If he or she does, Team A scores a point and you give student 3A a clue for which you expect another correct response. Continue giving Team A clues until some team member makes an incorrect response. An incorrect response sends the game back to the jumbled-word face-off, this time with students 2A and 2B. Instead of repeating giving clues to the first few students of each team, continue with the student after the one who gave the last incorrect response on the team. For example, if Team B wins the jumbled-word face-off and student 5B gave the last incorrect answer for Team B, you would start this round of clue questions with student 6B, and so on.

Lesson Twenty-three

Objective
To test the students' understanding of the main ideas and themes in **Homecoming**

Activities
Distribute the unit tests. Go over the instructions in detail and allow the students the entire class period to complete the exam. Then collect all test papers and assigned books prior to the end of the class period.

NOTES ABOUT THE UNIT TESTS IN THIS UNIT
Five different unit tests follow.

The **two short answer unit tests** are based primarily on facts from the novel and are followed by answer keys. Both have matching sections. The first test includes quotations (tell the significance of the quotation); the second has an essay section. Both contain a vocabulary section. Answers are given for all but the significance part of the quotations since these responses will be subjective.

The **one advanced short answer unit test** is based on the extra discussion questions and also contains an essay. Use the matching key for Short Answer Test #2 to check the correlating section of the advanced short answer test. There is no key for the short answer questions or the essay.

There are **two multiple choice unit tests**. Both have matching and vocabulary sections. The first test uses quotations (name only the speaker); the second requires an essay. Following the two unit tests is an answer sheet on which students should mark their answers. The same answer sheet should be used for both tests. Following the students' answer sheet for the multiple choice tests are the answer keys.

For the short answer vocabulary sections, choose ten of the vocabulary words from this unit, read them orally, and have the students write them down. Then, either have students write a definition or use the words in sentences.

Use these words for the vocabulary section of the advanced short answer test:

| mirth | raucous | exasperated | meandered | askew |
| conjecture | circuitous | cacophony | interspersed | turgid |

UNIT TESTS

Short Answer Unit Test #1
Homecoming

I. Matching/Identify

___ Sammy A. Dicey's father

___ Miss Eunice Logan B. owner of the circus

___ Louis C. one of the teenage runaways

___ Cynthia Voigt D. author of the book

___ Windy E. college student who helps Dicey

___ Liza Tillerman F. Dicey's brother

___ Francis Verricker G. Dicey's cousin

___ Will Hawkins H. Dicey's mother

II. Short Answer

1. Why was the Tillerman family traveling to Bridgeport?

2. Where is the children's father?

3. What did Sammy bring back to the campsite that Dicey made him return?

4. What did James do in the dormitory room that made Dicey feel ashamed?

5. What emotion did Dicey say that Cousin Eunice felt for the Tillerman children?

6. What news does Sergeant Gordo bring about Dicey's mother?

Short Answer Unit Test #1 continued page 2

7. What does Dicey figure was the expense of staying with Cousin Eunice?

8. What was the word that occurred to Dicey to describe her first view of her grandmother's farm?

9. What was the children's first project at their grandmother's farm?

10. What presents did the children receive when Will and Claire visited the farm?

III. Quotations: Tell the significance of the quotation.
1. "It runs in families. Hereditary craziness."

2. "…He'd call me his little only. I don't know why."

3. "We are family, aren't we? And when I think of you, all alone—abandoned—like myself really, in a way….."

4. "…It will be hard to place Maybeth. A retarded child—"

5. "I had a dream that you were all on a bus and the door closed and I couldn't get on. I ran and ran after it, but it kept getting away."

6. "It was eating the biscuits!" she cried. "He couldn't get it to chase us because it was hungry. Doesn't that serve him right."

7. "And I've been chased by dogs myself often enough not to be overly scared of them. Animal dogs or human dogs."

Short Answer Unit Test #1 continued page 3

8. "You're a little bit of my life now. You can't get away, and I can't get rid of you. That's a fact."

9. "Crazy as a coot, that's my opinion. We leave her alone. You should too."

10. "I know who you are. You hear me. I know who you are, and you can't stay here."

IV. Listen to the vocabulary word and spell it. After you have spelled all the words, go back and write down the definitions.

1.

2.

3.

4.

5.

6.

7.

8.

9.

10.

Key: Short Answer Unit Test #1
Homecoming

I. Matching/Identify

_F_	Sammy	A.	Dicey's father
_G_	Miss Eunice Logan	B.	owner of the circus
_C_	Louis	C.	one of the teenage runaways
_D_	Cynthia Voigt	D.	author of the book
_E_	Windy	E.	college student who helps Dicey
_H_	Liza Tillerman	F.	Dicey's brother
_A_	Francis Verricker	G.	Dicey's cousin
_B_	Will Hawkins	H.	Dicey's mother

II. Short Answer

1. Why was the Tillerman family traveling to Bridgeport?
   They were going to Aunt Cilla's house for help.

2. Where is the children's father?
   Their father left the family years earlier

3. What did Sammy bring back to the campsite that Dicey made him return?
   Sammy brought a wallet with twenty dollars in it.

4. What did James do in the dormitory room that made Dicey feel ashamed?
   James stole money from Stewart.

5. What emotion did Dicey say that Cousin Eunice felt for the Tillerman children?
   Dicey said she felt pity.

6. What news does Sergeant Gordo bring about Dicey's mother?
   She is in a catatonic state in a mental hospital in Massachusetts.

Key: Short Answer Unit Test #1 continued page 2

7. What does Dicey figure was the expense of staying with Cousin Eunice?
   She figures it is the cost of always being grateful.

8. What was the word that occurred to Dicey to describe her first view of her grandmother's farm?
   The word that occurred to her was "abandoned."

9. What was the children's first project at their grandmother's farm?
   They decided to pull down the honeysuckle vines.

10. What presents did the children receive when Will and Claire visited the farm?
    The children each received a bicycle.

III. Quotations: Tell the significance of the quotation.
   (**Note to the teacher:** Answers will of course vary. For your convenience, the speaker of the quotation is noted in each case.)

1. "It runs in families. Hereditary craziness."
   (James Tillerman)

2. "…He'd call me his little only. I don't know why."
   (Dicey Tillerman)

3. "We are family, aren't we? And when I think of you, all alone—abandoned—like myself really, in a way….."
   (Cousin Eunice Logan)

4. "…It will be hard to place Maybeth. A retarded child—"
   (Father Joseph)

5. "I had a dream that you were all on a bus and the door closed and I couldn't get on. I ran and ran after it, but it kept getting away."
   (Sammy Tillerman)

6. "It was eating the biscuits!" she cried. "He couldn't get it to chase us because it was hungry. Doesn't that serve him right."
   (Dicey Tillerman)

Key: Short Answer Unit Test #1 continued page 3

7. "And I've been chased by dogs myself often enough not to be overly scared of them. Animal dogs or human dogs."
(Will Hawkins)

8. "You're a little bit of my life now. You can't get away, and I can't get rid of you. That's a fact."
(Will Hawkins)

9. "Crazy as a coot, that's my opinion. We leave her alone. You should too."
(Millie the butcher)

10. "I know who you are. You hear me. I know who you are, and you can't stay here."
(Dicey's grandmother)

IV. Choose ten of the vocabulary words to read orally for the vocabulary section of this test.

1.

2.

3.

4.

5.

6.

7.

8.

9.

10.

Short Answer Unit Test #2
Homecoming

I. Matching/Identify

___ Sammy   A. Dicey's cousin

___ Miss Eunice Logan   B. Dicey's mother

___ Louis   C. owner of the circus

___ Cynthia Voigt   D. author of the book

___ Windy   E. one of the teenage runaways

___ Liza Tillerman   F. Dicey's brother

___ Francis Verricker   G. college student who helps Dicey

___ Will Hawkins   H. Dicey's father

II. Short Answer

1. Who is Peggy-o?

2. Why do the children stay so long at Rockland?

3. What does James say is the only true, unchanging thing?

4. What does Dicey learn from Cousin Eunice about her grandmother?

5. What does Cousin Eunice do every morning at 6:30?

6. What does Sister Berenice suggest to Dicey about Maybeth?

7. Who saved the children from Mr. Rudyard?

Short Answer Unit Test #2 continued page 2

8. What surprising thing did Dicey find in her grandmother's barn?

9. What major concession does the children's grandmother make at the dock?

10. What special question did Dicey ask her grandmother at the end of the book?

III. Essay
Name three themes in **Homecoming** and explain how each is developed.

Short Answer Unit Test #2 continued page 3

IV. Vocabulary

Listen to the vocabulary words and spell them. After you have spelled all the words, go back and write down the definitions.

1.

2.

3.

4.

5.

6.

7.

8.

9.

10.

Key: Short Answer Unit Test #2
Homecoming

I. Matching/Identify

_F_	Sammy	A.	Dicey's cousin
_A_	Miss Eunice Logan	B.	Dicey's mother
_E_	Louis	C.	owner of the circus
_D_	Cynthia Voigt	D.	author of the book
_G_	Windy	E.	one of the teenage runaways
_B_	Liza Tillerman	F.	Dicey's brother
_H_	Francis Verricker	G.	college student who helps Dicey
_C_	Will Hawkins	H.	Dicey's father

II. Short Answer

1. Who is Peggy-o?
   She is a character in a song that the children's mother taught them.

2. Why do the children stay so long at Rockland?
   They stay while James recuperates from his fall.

3. What does James say is the only true, unchanging thing?
   He says it is the speed of light.

4. What does Dicey learn from Cousin Eunice about her grandmother?
   She learns that her grandmother lives in Crisfield on the Eastern Shore of Maryland.

5. What does Cousin Eunice do every morning at 6:30?
   She goes to mass.

6. What does Sister Berenice suggest to Dicey about Maybeth?
   Sister Berenice thinks that Maybeth should be in a special school for the disabled.

Key: Short Answer Unit Test #2 continued page 2

7. Who saved the children from Mr. Rudyard?
   The people with the circus did.

8. What surprising thing did Dicey find in her grandmother's barn?
   She found a sailboat.

9. What major concession does the children's grandmother make at the dock?
   She says that the children can stay with her.

10. What special question did Dicey ask her grandmother at the end of the book?
    She asks if they could fix the sailboat up and have it.

III. Essay
   Name three themes in **Homecoming** and explain how each is developed.

IV. Vocabulary
   Choose ten of the vocabulary words to read orally for the vocabulary section of the test.

Advanced Short Answer Unit Test
Homecoming

I. Matching/Identify

   ____ Sammy   A. Dicey's cousin

   ____ Miss Eunice Logan B. Dicey's mother

   ____ Louis   C. owner of the circus

   ____ Cynthia Voigt   D. author of the book

   ____ Windy   E. one of the teenage runaways

   ____ Liza Tillerman   F. Dicey's brother

   ____ Francis Verricker G. college student who helps Dicey

   ____ Will Hawkins   H. Dicey's father

II. Short Answer

1. Are the characters in the story realistic? Explain.

2. How is repetition used in the novel? What is the purpose of repeating certain descriptions and phrases? Give specific examples to explain your thoughts.

3. Do the Tillerman children grow during the book, or are they about the same at the end as they were at the beginning? Explain your answer.

Advanced Short Answer Unit Test continued page 2

4. What do you think Cynthia Voigt's feelings are about children?

5. What does the open water symbolize for Dicey?

III. Essay
Using three separate characters in **Homecoming** (you may not use more than one of the Tillerman children), explain what "home" means to each.

Advanced Short Answer Unit Test continued page 3

IV. Vocabulary
Listen to the vocabulary words and write them down. After you have written down all the words, write a paragraph in which you use all the words. The paragraph must in some way relate to **Homecoming.**

1.

2.

3.

4.

5.

6.

7.

8.

9.

10.

<u>Paragraph</u>

Multiple Choice-Matching Unit Test #1
Homecoming

I. Matching/Identify

___ Sammy   A. Dicey's father

___ Miss Eunice Logan   B. owner of the circus

___ Louis   C. one of the teenage runaways

___ Cynthia Voigt   D. author of the book

___ Windy   E. college student who helps Dicey

___ Liza Tillerman   F. Dicey's brother

___ Francis Verricker   G. Dicey's cousin

___ Will Hawkins   H. Dicey's mother

II. Multiple Choice
1. Why was the Tillerman family traveling to Bridgeport?
    a. They had just bought a new home there.
    b. Dicey thought her father might be living there.
    c. Dicey's mother had some good friends there.
    d. They were going to Aunt Cilla's house for help.

2. Where is the children's father?
    a. He left them years earlier.
    b. He is living in New York City.
    c. He died just before Maybeth was born.
    d. He lives with his new family in Georgia.

3. What did Sammy bring back to the campsite that Dicey made him return?
    a. Two cheese sandwiches
    b. A wallet with twenty dollars in it
    c. A small brown dog
    d. An ID card that he found nearby

Multiple Choice Unit Test #1 continued page 2

4. What did James do in the dormitory room that made Dicey feel ashamed?
   a. He yelled at Windy.
   b. He told lies to everyone.
   c. He refused to help clean up the room.
   d. He stole money from Stewart.

5. What emotion did Dicey say that Cousin Eunice felt for the Tillerman children?
   a. Love
   b. Sympathy
   c. Empathy
   d. Pity

6. What news does Sergeant Gordo bring about Dicey's mother?
   a. That her mother has been found dead
   b. That her mother is back home in Provincetown
   c. That her mother is in a catatonic state in a mental hospital in Massachusetts
   d. That his investigation shows that her mother is living in Maryland

7. What does Dicey figure was the expense of staying with Cousin Eunice?
   a. Nearly a hundred dollars
   b. Her loss of pride
   c. The cost of always being grateful
   d. Her dignity

8. What was the word that occurred to Dicey to describe her first view of her grandmother's farm?
   a. Neat
   b. Abandoned
   c. Forlorn
   d. Beautiful

9. What was the children's first project at their grandmother's farm?
   a. Repairing the sailboat
   b. Canning
   c. Pulling down the honeysuckle vines
   d. Cleaning the inside of the house

Multiple Choice Unit Test #1 continued page 3

10. What presents did the children receive when Will and Claire visited the farm?
    a. Free circus tickets
    b. A kitten
    c. Bicycles
    d. New underwear

III. Quotations: Matching

A James B Dicey C Father Joseph D Sammy E Abigail Tillerman F Millie G Will H Eunice

1. "It runs in families. Hereditary craziness."

2. "…He'd call me his little only. I don't know why."

3. "We are family, aren't we? And when I think of you, all alone—abandoned—like myself really, in a way….."

4. "…It will be hard to place Maybeth. A retarded child—"

5. "I had a dream that you were all on a bus and the door closed and I couldn't get on. I ran and ran after it, but it kept getting away."

6. "It was eating the biscuits!" she cried. "He couldn't get it to chase us because it was hungry. Doesn't that serve him right."

7. "And I've been chased by dogs myself often enough not to be overly scared of them. Animal dogs or human dogs."

8. "You're a little bit of my life now. You can't get away, and I can't get rid of you. That's a fact."

9. "Crazy as a coot, that's my opinion. We leave her alone. You should too."

10. "I know who you are. You hear me. I know who you are, and you can't stay here."

Multiple Choice Unit Test continued page 4

IV. Vocabulary (Matching)

1.	succeeded	A.	beat
2.	pummeled	B.	a small open boat; rowboat
3.	solitude	C.	properly; precisely
4.	secluded	D.	glowed
5.	dinghy	E.	came after
6.	glimpse	F.	state of being alone
7.	meandered	G.	rumpled; disheveled
8.	lulled	H.	set apart
9.	conjecture	I.	rubbed
10.	primly	J.	moved aimlessly and idly
11.	circuitous	K.	promised solemnly; pledged
12.	hustled	L.	soothed
13.	vowed	M.	see briefly
14.	surged	N.	signs
15.	cacophony	O.	guesswork
16.	traipsed	P.	roundabout
17.	signals	Q.	hurried along
18.	chafed	R.	moved up quickly
19.	tousled	S.	jarring, discordant sound
20.	gleamed	T.	walked

Multiple Choice-Matching Unit Test #2

I. Matching/Identify

___ Sammy   A. Dicey's cousin

___ Miss Eunice Logan   B. Dicey's mother

___ Louis   C. owner of the circus

___ Cynthia Voigt   D. author of the book

___ Windy   E. one of the teenage runaways

___ Liza Tillerman   F. Dicey's brother

___ Francis Verricker   G. college student who helps Dicey

___ Will Hawkins   H. Dicey's father

II. Short Answer
1. Who is Peggy-o?
    a. The children's mother's best friend
    b. A character in a song that the children's mother taught them
    c. The children's mother's sister
    d. A friend from the Tillermans' old neighborhood

2. Why do the children stay so long at Rockland?
    a. Because it is so beautiful there
    b. Because Dicey can't make up her mind which way to go next
    c. Because Maybeth gets sick
    d. Because James is recuperating from a fall

3. What does James say is the only true, unchanging thing?
    a. The speed of light
    b. His mother's love for him
    c. His intellect
    d. His belief in God

Multiple Choice Unit Test #2 continued page 2

4. What does Dicey learn from Cousin Eunice about her grandmother?
    a. That her grandmother has died
    b. That her grandmother was too ill to see anyone
    c. that her grandmother lives in Crisfield on the Eastern Shore of Maryland
    d. That her grandmother had just moved out of the United States

5. What does Cousin Eunice do every morning at 6:30?
    a. She says a prayer for her mother.
    b. She goes to mass.
    c. She phones her mother.
    d. She leaves to go to work.

6. What does Sister Berenice suggest to Dicey about Maybeth?
    a. She thinks that Maybeth should be in a special school for the disabled.
    b. She thinks that Maybeth should be in third grade.
    c. She thinks Maybeth is really an adopted child.
    d. She thinks Maybeth is one of the sweetest children she has ever met.

7. Who saved the children from Mr. Rudyard?
    a. Louis and Edie
    b. The police
    c. Some passing motorists
    d. The people with the circus

8. What surprising thing did Dicey find in her grandmother's barn?
    a. A dead body
    b. A sailboat
    c. An old car
    d. A whole litter of kittens

9. What major concession does the children's grandmother make at the dock?
    a. That she really doesn't hate all children
    b. That the children can stay with her
    c. That she will phone Cousin Eunice
    d. that she will let the children pull all of the honeysuckle down

Multiple Choice Unit Test #2 continued page 3

10. What special question did Dicey ask her grandmother at the end of the book?
 a. If she could fix dinner that night
 b. If she could fix the sailboat up and have it
 c. If Maybeth could have her own room
 d. If James could go away to school

III. Essay
Name three themes in **Homecoming** and explain how each is developed.

Multiple Choice Unit Test #2 continued page 4

IV. Vocabulary (Matching)

1.	succeeded	A.	set apart
2.	pummeled	B.	properly; precisely
3.	solitude	C.	a small open boat; rowboat
4.	secluded	D.	promised solemnly; pledged
5.	dinghy	E.	see briefly
6.	glimpse	F.	state of being alone
7.	meandered	G.	rumpled; disheveled
8.	lulled	H.	came after
9.	conjecture	I.	rubbed
10.	primly	J.	moved aimlessly and idly
11.	circuitous	K.	glowed
12.	hustled	L.	soothed
13.	vowed	M.	beat
14.	surged	N.	hurried along
15.	cacophony	O.	guesswork
16.	traipsed	P.	roundabout
17.	signals	Q.	signs
18.	chafed	R.	walked
19.	tousled	S.	jarring, discordant sound
20.	gleamed	T.	moved up quickly

Keys to Multiple Choice Unit Tests

Test #1

Matching	Multiple Choice	Quotations	Vocabulary	
1 F	1 D	1 A	1 E	11 P
2 G	2 A	2 B	2 A	12 Q
3 C	3 B	3 H	3 F	13 K
4 D	4 D	4 C	4 G	14 R
5 E	5 D	5 D	5 B	15 S
6 H	6 C	6 B	6 M	16 T
7 A	7 C	7 G	7 J	17 N
8 B	8 B	8 G	8 L	18 I
	9 C	9 F	9 O	19 G
	10 C	10 E	10 C	20 D

Test #2

		Essay		
1 F	2 B		1 H	11 P
2 A	2 D		2 M	12 N
3 E	3 A		3 F	13 D
4 D	4 C		4 A	14 T
5 G	5 B		5 C	15 S
6 B	6 A		6 E	16 R
7 H	7 D		7 J	17 Q
8 C	8 B		8 L	18 I
	9 B		9 O	19 G
	10 B		10 B	20 K

UNIT RESOURCE MATERIALS

Bulletin Board Ideas
Homecoming

1. On the blackboard or, if you still have one free, the bulletin board, chart the course of the Tillerman children on a map. At every point where the children experienced some incident, put information about what happened there. You could use this method to chart just the people the Tillermans meet, or you could talk about how bad or how good the time spent there was for the children.

2. Cynthia Voigt has written several other books. Have students look in the school library for her books and try to get a sense of which each is about. Put some brightly colored paper on the bulletin board and have students write the name of one Cynthia Voigt book and one interesting piece of information about it. Encourage students to read all of the information posted so that perhaps they might get interested in reading one of the books.

3. Make a kind of writing mural out of one bulletin board in your classroom. Invite students to use the board to express their personal feelings about **Homecoming.** Ask students to take a minute at the beginning or end of each class period to write something that expresses their thoughts that day about the play, its ideas, its character, or its author. Set some guidelines about appropriateness of comments and then let students write whatever they want.

4. Save a portion of a black board to use as a bulletin board for rotating comments. Start each day with a comment that might be made by one of the characters in **Homecoming**. Sign your comment with the name of one of the characters. For example, you might write, "It's still true"—James Tillerman. Invite students to make comments about the one you put up and sign their comment with the name of one of the other three characters. Try to build up some suspense every day about what comment will appear from which character. None of the comments need be from the book, only in character for the person making it.

5. Make a bulletin board listing the vocabulary words for this unit. As you complete sections of the novel and discuss the vocabulary for each section, write the definitions on the bulletin board. Encourage students to look at the board often so that they learn the words easily.

6. With the permission of the student writers, post the best writing assignments done for this unit.

Bulletin Board Ideas continued page 2

7. If you have students who can draw, ask them to sketch a picture of one of the major characters or a scene from **Homecoming** and post it on the bulletin board.

8. Ask students to look through magazines and find pictures of people that look like their idea of any of the five characters in **Homecoming**. Get the students to post their pictures on the bulletin board labeled with the names of the characters the pictures make them think of. If you run short of material to cover one day, you could point to each picture on the bulletin board and see if there is consensus in the class about whether the pictures are like the characters or not. Even if the class disagrees with a particular association, that doesn't make the picture chosen wrong. It only means that a student has his or her own conception of what the character is like. Maybe that student will feel free to explain what he or she is thinking about the character. This might enlarge everyone's thoughts about the characters and the book.

Extra Activities Packet
Homecoming

One of the difficulties in teaching a book is that not all students read at the same speed. One student who likes to read may take the book home and finish it in a day or two. Sometimes a few students finish the in-class assignments early. The problem,. Then, is finding suitable extra activities for students.

One useful thing to do is to keep a little library in the classroom. For this unit on **Homecoming**, you might check out from the school or local library other related books and articles about mental illness, retardation, family ties, grandparents, travel, the Eastern Shore of Maryland, Annapolis, Maryland, child/parent relationships, sibling rivalry, crabbing, topics about the Chesapeake Bay, ships and shipping, etc. If possible, also have on hand some copies of Cynthia Voigt other works so that students can read something else by the author if they choose to do so.

Other things you may keep on hand are puzzles. There are some in this unit directly relating to **Homecoming**. Feel free to duplicate them for your students' use.

Some students may like to draw or paint. You might devise a contest or allow some extra-credit grade for students who draw characters or scenes from **Homecoming**. Note, too, that if the students do not want to keep their drawings, you may pick up some extra bulletin board materials this way. If you have a contest and you supply the prize (a CD, a copy of another work by Voigt a copy of a book on a subject similar to that in **Homecoming,** for example), you could possibly make the drawing itself a non-refundable entry fee. Make sure you assure students that you will continue to place their name on the board with the drawing. This can assure a student that years into the future his or her drawing will still be in his or her old classroom.

The pages which follow contain games, puzzles, and worksheets. The keys, when appropriate, immediately follow the puzzle or worksheet. There are two main groups of activities: one group for the unit; that is, generally relating to the text of **Homecoming**, and another group of activities related strictly to the vocabulary words in **Homecoming**.

Directions for these games, puzzles, and worksheets are self-explanatory. The object here is to provide you with extra materials you may use in any way you choose.

More Activities
Homecoming

1. Have students choose to "be" any of the main characters. Ask them to keep a journal daily in which they write about what happens to them—but in the voice and character of their chosen character. Everything they write in their journal, even if they want to make comments about class to you, should be done in character.

2. Encourage students to act out a few scenes of **Homecoming**. It is easy to adapt the chapters to dramatic form. Ask students to pretend that **Homecoming** is being made into a play or a film. Students could rehearse a few scenes

3. Encourage students to write a couple of paragraphs for the book from the standpoint of a character other than Dicey. For example, ask them to write a couple paragraphs from Maybeth's or Sammy's standpoint. Maybe they could write a few paragraphs from the standpoint of Cousin Eunice or their grandmother. The people and events will be the same, but they will be seen directly through the character's eyes. This kind of exercise will make students look at the details of the book differently than they did on a first reading.

4. Have students pretend to be one of the Tillerman children or perhaps Cousin Eunice or Abigail Tillerman and ask them to write letters to Cynthia Voigt. In the letters they should try to get Voigt rewrite all or parts of the novel in order to significantly change their role in the book.

5. Let interested students "teach" a class one day. If the number of interested students is sufficient, you could allow the students to work together, make a clear plan, and actually teach a whole class. Feel free to share your daily lesson plans with the students as they prepare to teach.

6. Have students design a book jacket or a CD cover for a book or a piece of music that they think Dicey, her mother, her grandmother, or one her siblings to create. They should name the piece of music and then design the cover in whatever way they think is appropriate.

7. Make a bulletin board with telephone numbers students can call for advice in case they want additional information about the subjects presented in **Homecoming.** For instance, if students wanted information about the Eastern Shore of Maryland, Crisfield in particular, Social Security support, foster families, travel, family relationships, etc. Students might want this information for purposes of class or even for real life situations.

More Activities continued page 2

8. Ask students to pretend that someone from outer space has been deposited into the middle of the action presented in **Homecoming**. The students could pretend to be the alien and write a letter back to their planet describing the new world that they are observing.

9. Have students assume that they have become friends with any one of the major characters (the Tillerman children, Cousin Eunice, Abigail Tillerman, The students should write a paper or have a discussion regarding the type of gift they would like to give to their chosen character and why.

10. Have students discuss which television show they believe would be the favorite of each of the major characters in the play.

11. Students could consider whether they would like to be Liza Tillerman's child or Abigail Tillerman's grandchild. Have them explain why or why not they believe either of the characters would be a good parent.

12. Students could create original costumes for one or two of the characters in **Homecoming**. A costume could actually be made and modeled or a few costume designs could be drawn and posted around the classroom.

Homecoming Word Search

```
P E G G Y R E T E M E C A R W I L L B
R W D T X L A J O F H X Z R R D Q I O
G A F R X O V V K M L D W G D P C M U
N L B Y B C T H D R A Y D U R Y L O L
B L D H Y R S N E N T T L G C U M N D
S E L L A I H E N Q N W O L F S Y E E
V T S W F X T Y P C E M E E G R X Y R
Z E E A S S B A R C M N T R L O G A N
T T R K M Z M I U R U A E E I C R N M
S G O R Y M S C O N R H W T G K E N X
M O T B I F Y M S G T Y I A H L E A D
B Q I C I C H Z A O M N N R T A N P S
W M L E C L K X M S W M D D M N S O Y
K C L R F A H E W K S G O E A D L L T
L D E X G I X M R R T W W D Y D E I T
B P R Y L R G B G X Z G S L B I E S G
L J M M J E H P C F K W G S E E V R V
K F A J O S E P H S T B N N T D E Y T
Z L N G R A N D M O T H E R H T S M D
```

ANNAPOLIS	DANNY	MASS	SAMMY
BICYCLE	DIED	MAYBETH	SOUR
BOAT	FISH	MENTAL	STEER
BOOKS	GRANDMOTHER	MONEY	STEWART
BOULDER	GRATEFUL	MOTHER	TILLERMAN
CAR	GREENSLEEVES	NUN	TOMATO
CEMETERY	JOSEPH	PEGGY	VERRICKER
CLAIRE	LIGHT	RETARDED	WALLET
CRABS	LOGAN	ROCKLAND	WILL
CRISFIELD	MAP	RUDYARD	WINDOWS

Homecoming Word Search Answer Key

```
P E G G Y R E T E M E C A R W I L L B
  W         A     O                 I   O
  A         O       M L D         C   M U
  L     B   T H D R A Y D U R Y L   O   L
  L     R   S   E   N   T     C     N   D
  E     A   I   E     N     O L F   E   E
V T S W F   T Y P C   M N T R     R   Y R
  E E A S S B A R C   M N T R L O G A N
  T R K M   M I   U   U A E E I C R   N
S   O R   M S   O   N R H W T G K E   N
    O T   I F Y M   S G T     I A H L E
  B I   I C   L   A O       N R T A N P
      L E L   K   M S       D D M N S O
        L   A     E         O E A D L L
      D E   I         S     W D Y D E I
          R R               S   B I E S
          M E                   E E V
            A J O S E P H       T D E
            N G R A N D M O T H E R H S
```

ANNAPOLIS	DANNY	MASS	SAMMY
BICYCLE	DIED	MAYBETH	SOUR
BOAT	FISH	MENTAL	STEER
BOOKS	GRANDMOTHER	MONEY	STEWART
BOULDER	GRATEFUL	MOTHER	TILLERMAN
CAR	GREENSLEEVES	NUN	TOMATO
CEMETERY	JOSEPH	PEGGY	VERRICKER
CLAIRE	LIGHT	RETARDED	WALLET
CRABS	LOGAN	ROCKLAND	WILL
CRISFIELD	MAP	RUDYARD	WINDOWS

Homecoming Crossword

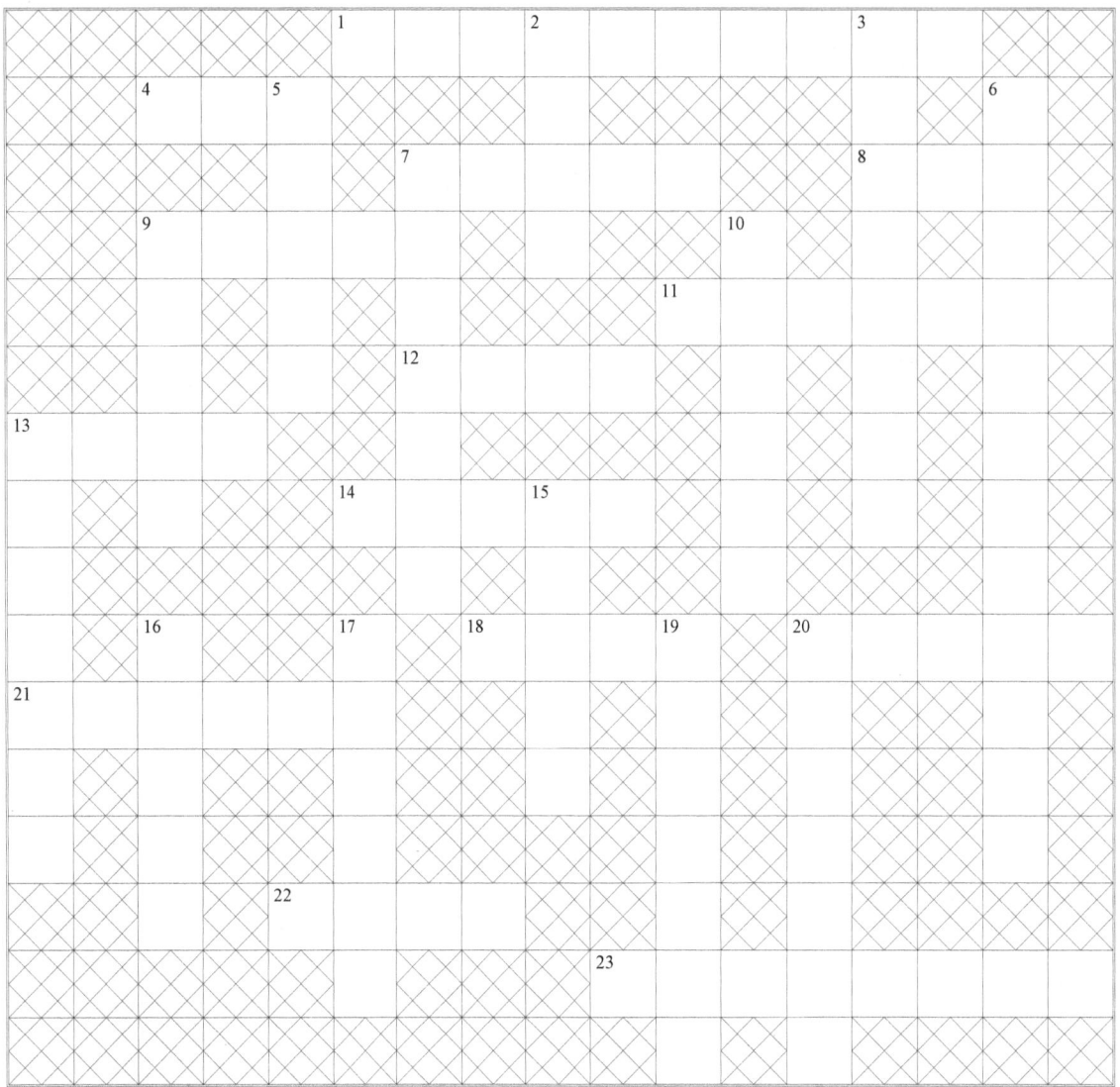

Across
1. City where Aunt Cilla lived
4. The children ate at McDonalds and bought a ___ in Fairfield
7. Jerry allows Dicey to do ___ the boat
8. Dicey got $57 for the sale of her mother's
9. James says the only true, unchanging thing is the speed of ___
11. James fell off one at Rockland State Park
12. He drove the children to Crisfield
13. Dicey found one in the barn
14. The Tillerman children learn to eat these at their grandmother's house
18. Kind of expression Dicey's grandmother's picture had
20. Lou & Edie stole this from Edie's father
21. She ran off Mr. Rudyard & rescued the children
22. Cousin Eunice goes to this every morning at 6:30
23. Dicey figures the expense of staying with cousin Eunice is the cost of always being this

Down
2. Eunice told the children that Aunt Cilla had ___
3. The children ate mussels & clams at this state park
5. Character in a song the children's mother taught them: ___-O
6. Song Maybeth sang with Stewart
7. James stole money from him in the dormitory room
9. Eunice's last name
10. Father ___: Cousin Eunice's friend & spiritual counselor
13. Each child received one when Will & Claire visited the farm
15. Grandmother said her husband used these to build a wall to keep things out
16. The mall guard, Lou & Edie believe dicey is a boy named ___
17. Kind of hospital Dicey's mother is in, in Massachusetts
19. He chased the children with his dogs
20. Persuades Sammy to start walking to Bridgeport

Homecoming Crossword Answer Key

					¹B	R	I	D	G	E	P	O	³R	T	
		⁴M	A	⁵P			I						O		⁶G
				E		⁷S	T	E	E	R		⁸C	A	R
		⁹L	I	G	H	T	D			¹⁰J		K		E
		O				E		¹¹B	O	U	L	D	E	R
		G		Y		¹²W	I	L	L		S		A	N
¹³B	O	A	T			A				E		N		S
I		N		¹⁴C	R	¹⁵A	B	S		P		D		L
C				T		S		O		H				E
Y	¹⁶D		¹⁷M	¹⁸S	O	U	R		¹⁹R	²⁰M	O	N	E	Y
²¹C	L	A	I	R	E		K		U	A		V	
L	N		N		S		D	Y		E		
E	N		T				Y	B		S		
	Y		²²M	A	S	S		A	E			
				L		²³G	R	A	T	E	F	U	L
						D	H						

Across
1. City where Aunt Cilla lived
4. The children ate at McDonalds and bought a __ in Fairfield
7. Jerry allows Dicey to do __ the boat
8. Dicey got $57 for the sale of her mother's
9. James says the only true, unchanging thing is the speed of __
11. James fell off one at Rockland State Park
12. He drove the children to Crisfield
13. Dicey found one in the barn
14. The Tillerman children learn to eat these at their grandmother's house
18. Kind of expression Dicey's grandmother's picture had
20. Lou & Edie stole this from Edie's father
21. She ran off Mr. Rudyard & rescued the children
22. Cousin Eunice goes to this every morning at 6:30
23. Dicey figures the expense of staying with cousin Eunice is the cost of always being this

Down
2. Eunice told the children that Aunt Cilla had ___
3. The children ate mussels & clams at this state park
5. Character in a song the children's mother taught them: ___-O
6. Song Maybeth sang with Stewart
7. James stole money from him in the dormitory room
9. Eunice's last name
10. Father ___: Cousin Eunice's friend & spiritual counselor
13. Each child received one when Will & Claire visited the farm
15. Grandmother said her husband used these to build a wall to keep things out
16. The mall guard, Lou & Edie believe dicey is a boy named ___
17. Kind of hospital Dicey's mother is in, in Massachusetts
19. He chased the children with his dogs
20. Persuades Sammy to start walking to Bridgeport

MATCHING QUIZ/WORKSHEET 1 - Homecoming

___ 1. PEGGY   A. Kind of hospital Dicey's mother is in, in Massachusetts

___ 2. JOSEPH   B. Kind of expression Dicey's grandmother's picture had

___ 3. NUN   C. Family name for Dicey & siblings

___ 4. ROCKLAND   D. Father ___: Cousin Eunice's friend & spiritual counselor

___ 5. MAP   E. Jerry allows Dicey to do ___ the boat.

___ 6. CEMETERY   F. She ran off Mr. Rudyard & rescued the children.

___ 7. WINDOWS   G. He drove the children to Crisfield.

___ 8. MAYBETH   H. Word Fr. Joseph applies to Maybeth in his discussion with Dicey

___ 9. MOTHER   I. The storekeeper in St. Michaels sounded like Dicey's ___.

___10. CLAIRE   J. Cousin Eunice must abandon her plans for becoming one.

___11. BOOKS   K. James stole money from him in the dormitory room.

___12. BOAT   L. City where Aunt Cilla lived

___13. BRIDGEPORT   M. Dicey decides to go to Crisfield to meet her ___.

___14. WILL   N. Persuades Sammy to start walking to Bridgeport

___15. SOUR   O. Dicey's long-missing father's name: Francis ___

___16. MASS   P. Grandmother said her husband used these to build a wall to keep things out.

___17. RETARDED   Q. He chased the children with his dogs.

___18. RUDYARD   R. Dicey found one in the barn.

___19. TILLERMAN   S. Cousin Eunice goes to this every morning at 6:30.

___20. STEWART   T. Character in a song the children's mother taught them: ___-O

___21. STEER   U. The children ate mussels & clams at this state park.

___22. GRANDMOTHER   V. Where the children slept after rowing across the river

___23. VERRICKER   W. Dicey got a job washing them.

___24. MENTAL   X. The children ate at McDonalds and bought a ___ in Fairfield.

___25. FISH   Y. Sammy caught them at Rockland State Park.

KEY: MATCHING QUIZ/WORKSHEET 1 - Homecoming

T - 1. PEGGY		A. Kind of hospital Dicey's mother is in, in Massachusetts
D - 2. JOSEPH		B. Kind of expression Dicey's grandmother's picture had
J - 3. NUN		C. Family name for Dicey & siblings
U - 4. ROCKLAND		D. Father ___: Cousin Eunice's friend & spiritual counselor
X - 5. MAP		E. Jerry allows Dicey to do ___ the boat.
V - 6. CEMETERY		F. She ran off Mr. Rudyard & rescued the children.
W - 7. WINDOWS		G. He drove the children to Crisfield.
N - 8. MAYBETH		H. Word Fr. Joseph applies to Maybeth in his discussion with Dicey
I - 9. MOTHER		I. The storekeeper in St. Michaels sounded like Dicey's ___.
F - 10. CLAIRE		J. Cousin Eunice must abandon her plans for becoming one.
P - 11. BOOKS		K. James stole money from him in the dormitory room.
R - 12. BOAT		L. City where Aunt Cilla lived
L - 13. BRIDGEPORT		M. Dicey decides to go to Crisfield to meet her ___.
G - 14. WILL		N. Persuades Sammy to start walking to Bridgeport
B - 15. SOUR		O. Dicey's long-missing father's name: Francis ___
S - 16. MASS		P. Grandmother said her husband used these to build a wall to keep things out.
H - 17. RETARDED		Q. He chased the children with his dogs.
Q - 18. RUDYARD		R. Dicey found one in the barn.
C - 19. TILLERMAN		S. Cousin Eunice goes to this every morning at 6:30.
K - 20. STEWART		T. Character in a song the children's mother taught them: ___-O
E - 21. STEER		U. The children ate mussels & clams at this state park.
M - 22. GRANDMOTHER		V. Where the children slept after rowing across the river
O - 23. VERRICKER		W. Dicey got a job washing them.
A - 24. MENTAL		X. The children ate at McDonalds and bought a ___ in Fairfield.
Y - 25. FISH		Y. Sammy caught them at Rockland State Park.

MATCHING QUIZ/WORKSHEET 2 - Homecoming

___ 1. BOULDER A. The mall guard, Lou, & Edie believe Dicey is a boy named ____.

___ 2. JOSEPH B. James stole money from him in the dormitory room.

___ 3. CAR C. Word Fr. Joseph applies to Maybeth in his discussion with Dicey

___ 4. STEER D. Dicey got $57 for the sale of her mother's.

___ 5. ROCKLAND E. Persuades Sammy to start walking to Bridgeport

___ 6. CEMETERY F. Sammy caught them at Rockland State Park.

___ 7. STEWART G. Jerry allows Dicey to do ___ the boat.

___ 8. RETARDED H. Abigail Tillerman lives there.

___ 9. FISH I. The children decide to make money by becoming ___ pickers.

___ 10. MAYBETH J. Where the children slept after rowing across the river

___ 11. CRISFIELD K. He drove the children to Crisfield.

___ 12. TOMATO L. Father ___: Cousin Eunice's friend & spiritual counselor

___ 13. ANNAPOLIS M. The children met Jerry & Tom at a boatyard there.

___ 14. MENTAL N. City where Aunt Cilla lived

___ 15. DANNY O. Kind of hospital Dicey's mother is in, in Massachusetts

___ 16. PEGGY P. The storekeeper in St. Michaels sounded like Dicey's ___.

___ 17. LOGAN Q. James says the only true, unchanging thing is the speed of ___.

___ 18. BICYCLE R. Dicey got a job washing them.

___ 19. WILL S. Character in a song the children's mother taught them: ___-O

___ 20. WALLET T. James fell off one at Rockland State Park.

___ 21. MOTHER U. Eunice's last name

___ 22. GRATEFUL V. Each child received one when Will & Claire visited the farm.

___ 23. BRIDGEPORT W. The children ate mussels & clams at this state park.

___ 24. WINDOWS X. Dicey made Sammy return the ___ he stole that had $20 in it.

___ 25. LIGHT Y. Dicey figures the expense of staying with cousin Eunice is the cost of always being this.

KEY: MATCHING QUIZ/WORKSHEET 2 - Homecoming

T - 1.	BOULDER	A. The mall guard, Lou, & Edie believe Dicey is a boy named ____.
L - 2.	JOSEPH	B. James stole money from him in the dormitory room.
D - 3.	CAR	C. Word Fr. Joseph applies to Maybeth in his discussion with Dicey
G - 4.	STEER	D. Dicey got $57 for the sale of her mother's.
W - 5.	ROCKLAND	E. Persuades Sammy to start walking to Bridgeport
J - 6.	CEMETERY	F. Sammy caught them at Rockland State Park.
B - 7.	STEWART	G. Jerry allows Dicey to do ___ the boat.
C - 8.	RETARDED	H. Abigail Tillerman lives there.
F - 9.	FISH	I. The children decide to make money by becoming ___ pickers.
E - 10.	MAYBETH	J. Where the children slept after rowing across the river
H - 11.	CRISFIELD	K. He drove the children to Crisfield.
I - 12.	TOMATO	L. Father ___: Cousin Eunice's friend & spiritual counselor
M - 13.	ANNAPOLIS	M. The children met Jerry & Tom at a boatyard there.
O - 14.	MENTAL	N. City where Aunt Cilla lived
A - 15.	DANNY	O. Kind of hospital Dicey's mother is in, in Massachusetts
S - 16.	PEGGY	P. The storekeeper in St. Michaels sounded like Dicey's ___.
U - 17.	LOGAN	Q. James says the only true, unchanging thing is the speed of ___.
V - 18.	BICYCLE	R. Dicey got a job washing them.
K - 19.	WILL	S. Character in a song the children's mother taught them: ___-O
X - 20.	WALLET	T. James fell off one at Rockland State Park.
P - 21.	MOTHER	U. Eunice's last name
Y - 22.	GRATEFUL	V. Each child received one when Will & Claire visited the farm.
N - 23.	BRIDGEPORT	W. The children ate mussels & clams at this state park.
R - 24.	WINDOWS	X. Dicey made Sammy return the ___ he stole that had $20 in it.
Q - 25.	LIGHT	Y. Dicey figures the expense of staying with cousin Eunice is the cost of always being this.

JUGGLE LETTER REVIEW GAME CLUE SHEET - Homecoming

1. DARYDRU = 1. _____
   He chased the children with his dogs.

2. IYCBCLE = 2. _____
   Each child received one when Will & Claire visited the farm.

3. REPDTOIRBG = 3. _____
   City where Aunt Cilla lived

4. SDWONIW = 4. _____
   Dicey got a job washing them.

5. RCEEMYET = 5. _____
   Where the children slept after rowing across the river

6. NDANY = 6. _____
   The mall guard, Lou, & Edie believe Dicey is a boy named ____.

7. EVSLENESEGRE = 7. _____
   Song Maybeth sang with Stewart

8. AGONL = 8. _____
   Eunice's last name

9. SCARB = 9. _____
   The Tillerman children learn to eat these at their grandmother's house.

10. DRDARTEE =10. _____
    Word Fr. Joseph applies to Maybeth in his discussion with Dicey

11. LILW =11. _____
    He drove the children to Crisfield.

12. PINNAALOS =12. _____
    The children met Jerry & Tom at a boatyard there.

13. PGYGE =13. _____
    Character in a song the children's mother taught them: ___-O

14. MLELNITRA =14. _____
    Family name for Dicey & siblings

15. AMP =15. _____
    The children ate at McDonalds and bought a __ in Fairfield.

16. AMELTN =16. _____
Kind of hospital Dicey's mother is in, in Massachusetts

17. YAMSM =17. _____
He always argues with Dicey's decisions.

18. FLERGTAU =18. _____
Dicey figures the expense of staying with cousin Eunice is the cost of always being this.

19. SAMS =19. _____
Cousin Eunice goes to this every morning at 6:30.

20. GHTLI =20. _____
James says the only true, unchanging thing is the speed of ___.

21. IERRERCVK =21. _____
Dicey's long-missing father's name: Francis ___

22. OJSEPH =22. _____
Father ___: Cousin Eunice's friend & spiritual counselor

23. ABOT =23. _____
Dicey found one in the barn.

24. HMYEATB =24. _____
Persuades Sammy to start walking to Bridgeport

25. HFSI =25. _____
Sammy caught them at Rockland State Park.

26. DNKCOLRA =26. _____
The children ate mussels & clams at this state park.

27. EICRLA =27. _____
She ran off Mr. Rudyard & rescued the children.

28. LATWLE =28. _____
Dicey made Sammy return the ___ he stole that had $20 in it.

29. ENOYM =29. _____
Lou & Edie stole this from Edie's father.

30. ACR =30. _____
Dicey got $57 for the sale of her mother's.

31. OKOSB =31. _____
Grandmother said her husband used these to build a wall to keep things out.

32. ROEBULD =32. _____
James fell off one at Rockland State Park.

33. UOSR =33. _____
Kind of expression Dicey's grandmother's picture had

34. TSRWETA =34. _____
James stole money from him in the dormitory room.

35. NUN =35. _____
Cousin Eunice must abandon her plans for becoming one.

36. TOMDREGRHAN =36. _____
Dicey decides to go to Crisfield to meet her ___.

37. HTMOER =37. _____
The storekeeper in St. Michaels sounded like Dicey's ___.

KEY: JUGGLE LETTER REVIEW GAME CLUE SHEET - Homecoming

1. DARYDRU = 1. RUDYARD
   He chased the children with his dogs.

2. IYCBCLE = 2. BICYCLE
   Each child received one when Will & Claire visited the farm.

3. REPDTOIRBG = 3. BRIDGEPORT
   City where Aunt Cilla lived

4. SDWONIW = 4. WINDOWS
   Dicey got a job washing them.

5. RCEEMYET = 5. CEMETERY
   Where the children slept after rowing across the river

6. NDANY = 6. DANNY
   The mall guard, Lou, & Edie believe Dicey is a boy named ____.

7. EVSLENESEGRE = 7. GREENSLEEVES
   Song Maybeth sang with Stewart

8. AGONL = 8. LOGAN
   Eunice's last name

9. SCARB = 9. CRABS
   The Tillerman children learn to eat these at their grandmother's house.

10. DRDARTEE =10. RETARDED
    Word Fr. Joseph applies to Maybeth in his discussion with Dicey

11. LILW =11. WILL
    He drove the children to Crisfield.

12. PINNAALOS =12. ANNAPOLIS
    The children met Jerry & Tom at a boatyard there.

13. PGYGE =13. PEGGY
    Character in a song the children's mother taught them: ____-O

14. MLELNITRA =14. TILLERMAN
    Family name for Dicey & siblings

15. AMP =15. MAP
    The children ate at McDonalds and bought a __ in Fairfield.

16. AMELTN   =16. MENTAL
              Kind of hospital Dicey's mother is in, in Massachusetts

17. YAMSM   =17. SAMMY
              He always argues with Dicey's decisions.

18. FLERGTAU =18. GRATEFUL
              Dicey figures the expense of staying with cousin Eunice is the cost of always being this.

19. SAMS   =19. MASS
              Cousin Eunice goes to this every morning at 6:30.

20. GHTLI   =20. LIGHT
              James says the only true, unchanging thing is the speed of ___.

21. IERRERCVK =21. VERRICKER
              Dicey's long-missing father's name: Francis ___

22. OJSEPH   =22. JOSEPH
              Father ___: Cousin Eunice's friend & spiritual counselor

23. ABOT   =23. BOAT
              Dicey found one in the barn.

24. HMYEATB   =24. MAYBETH
              Persuades Sammy to start walking to Bridgeport

25. HFSI   =25. FISH
              Sammy caught them at Rockland State Park.

26. DNKCOLRA =26. ROCKLAND
              The children ate mussels & clams at this state park.

27. EICRLA   =27. CLAIRE
              She ran off Mr. Rudyard & rescued the children.

28. LATWLE   =28. WALLET
              Dicey made Sammy return the ___ he stole that had $20 in it.

29. ENOYM   =29. MONEY
              Lou & Edie stole this from Edie's father.

30. ACR   =30. CAR
              Dicey got $57 for the sale of her mother's.

31. OKOSB =31. BOOKS

Grandmother said her husband used these to build a wall to keep things out.

32. ROEBULD =32. BOULDER

James fell off one at Rockland State Park.

33. UOSR =33. SOUR

Kind of expression Dicey's grandmother's picture had

34. TSRWETA =34. STEWART

James stole money from him in the dormitory room.

35. NUN =35. NUN

Cousin Eunice must abandon her plans for becoming one.

36. TOMDREGRHAN =36. GRANDMOTHER

Dicey decides to go to Crisfield to meet her ___.

37. HTMOER =37. MOTHER

The storekeeper in St. Michaels sounded like Dicey's ___.

VOCABULARY RESOURCE MATERIALS

Homecoming Vocabulary Word Search

```
F A L T E R E D I G R U T E E M I N G
C O C O O N Q E N E D Z E R J I H H V
M K P M P S L Q T P E L N E B R V M S
B G A Q D I T N E R G T U V K T C P L
F L R S G K U R N I R N O O S H O Z O
C U G A K A J A T M U E U L E F N D U
Y X R L S E R U P L S C S V C H T A C
D F D R I X W C R Y L S S E R R R B H
R E E P O M T O O G A E Y D E P A B E
U I R K R W P U D V N L C T T Z R L D
T R E S P A S S I N G A Z G I Z Y E Q
S E T Y J Y C Y E L I V W M V L N G S
O V S M C R P T E S S N M E E O L D L
L E U M A O S A E C T O C V D V V E I
E R L E F A M N H U B C V N M O A T R
M F F T E E M A O I P C A O C T G S D
N D N R D A F V L Q F B F P W Z U I N
L T B Y T E E E C F A T I G U E E O E
Y A Y K D D D E S R U P C R O W E D H T
```

ABANDONED	FRAGILE	SECRETIVE
ABREAST	FURROWS	SIGNALS
AMNESIA	GLEAMED	SLOUCHED
ARCS	GLIMPSE	SOLEMNLY
ASKEW	GNAWED	STURDY
CHAFED	HOISTED	SURGED
CLAMOR	IMMOBILE	SYMMETRY
COCOON	INTENT	TEEMING
COMA	MIRTH	TENDRILS
CONTRARY	MOAT	TENUOUS
CONVALESCENT	PRIMLY	TILLER
CROWED	PROD	TRESPASSING
DABBLE	PURSED	TURGID
DEVOUT	RAUCOUS	VAGUE
FALTERED	REVERIE	VOWED
FATIGUE	REVOLVED	ZIGZAG
FLUSTERED	SAUNTER	

Homecoming Vocabulary Word Search Answer Key

```
F A L T E R E D I G R U T E E M I N G
C O C O O N   E N E D   E R   I R   
    M   L T P E     N   E   T     S
    A   I N E R G T U V   I T C   L
F L   S G U R N I R N O O S H   O
C U G A K A   A T M U E U L   E N D U
Y   R L S E   U P L S C V C   T A C
D F D R I   W C R Y L S   E   R B H
R E E   O M   O O G A E   D   A B E
U I R     W P U D   N L   T   R L D
T R E S P A S S I N G A Z G I   Y E
S E T Y     C   E L I V W M V L N   S
O V S M C R   T E S S N M E E O   D L
L E U M A O S A E C T O     D   V E I
E R L   A M N H U B C V N M O A T R
M   F   T E E M A O I     A O     G S D
N     R D A F V L   B     W     U I N
L   B Y   E E   F A T I G U E   E O E
Y A     D D E S R U P C R O W E D H T
```

ABANDONED	FRAGILE	SECRETIVE
ABREAST	FURROWS	SIGNALS
AMNESIA	GLEAMED	SLOUCHED
ARCS	GLIMPSE	SOLEMNLY
ASKEW	GNAWED	STURDY
CHAFED	HOISTED	SURGED
CLAMOR	IMMOBILE	SYMMETRY
COCOON	INTENT	TEEMING
COMA	MIRTH	TENDRILS
CONTRARY	MOAT	TENUOUS
CONVALESCENT	PRIMLY	TILLER
CROWED	PROD	TRESPASSING
DABBLE	PURSED	TURGID
DEVOUT	RAUCOUS	VAGUE
FALTERED	REVERIE	VOWED
FATIGUE	REVOLVED	ZIGZAG
FLUSTERED	SAUNTER	

Homecoming Vocabulary Crossword

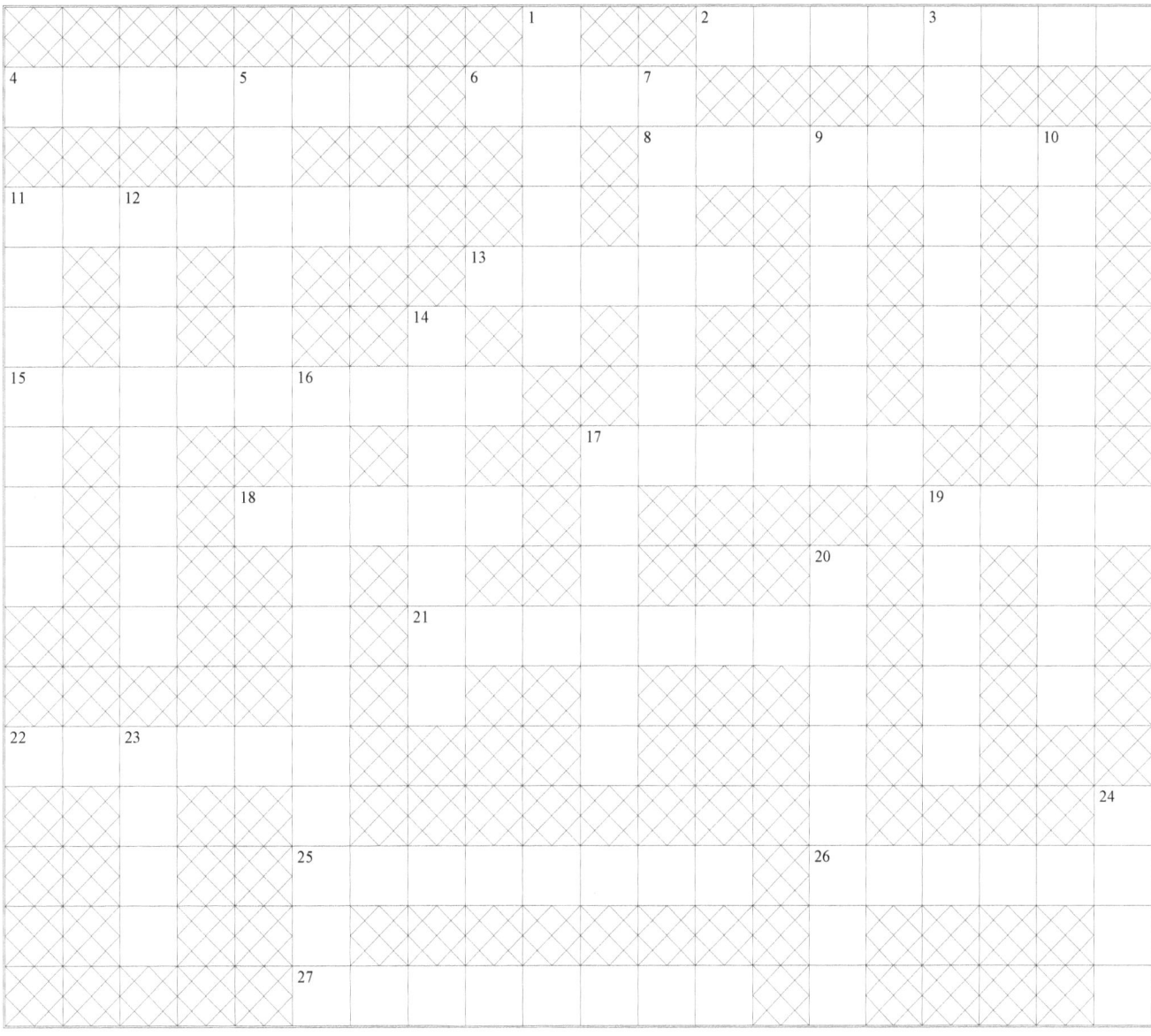

Across
2. Unmoving; fixed
4. Frowned
6. Deep, prolonged unconsciousness
8. Obedient; docile
11. Make a kind of bubbling sound
13. Promised solemnly; pledged
15. Moved aimlessly and idly
17. Strong; healthy
18. Lacking clear or distinct form
19. Wide ditch filled with water
21. Outrageous
22. Loud outcry
25. Walked
26. Lever that steers the boat
27. Became less

Down
1. Comfortable retreat; refuge
3. Moving about jerkily
5. Soothed
7. Side by side
9. Spoke in a monotonous tone
10. Expressed in greater detail
11. See briefly
12. Slow in development
14. Slight
16. Impatient
17. Moved up quickly; swelled
19. Gladness
20. Balanced or harmonious proportions
23. Shapes like curves
24. Goad to action

Homecoming Vocabulary Crossword Answer Key

							¹C		²I	M	M	³O	B	I	L	E
⁴S	C	O	W	⁵L	E	⁶D		⁷C	O	M	A					
				U				C			⁸B	⁹I	D	D	A	B	L	E
¹¹G	¹²U	R	G	L	E	D		O			R		D	R		B		L
L		E		L			¹³V	O	W	E	D			O		L		A
I		T		E		¹⁴T		N		A				N		N		B
¹⁵M	E	A	N	D	¹⁶E	R	E	D		S				E		G		O
P		R			X		N			¹⁷S	T	U	R	D	Y			R
¹⁸S	D			V	A	G	U	E		U				¹⁹M	O	A	T
E	E			I			S			O				²⁰S		I		T
	D			P			²¹U	N	N	G	O	D	L	Y		R		E
				E			S			E				M		T		D
²²C	²³L	A	M	O	R					D				M		H		
	R			A										E				²⁴P
	C			²⁵T	R	A	I	P	S	E	D		²⁶T	I	L	L	E	R
	S			E										R				O
				²⁷D	W	I	N	D	L	E	D			Y				D

Across
- 2. Unmoving; fixed
- 4. Frowned
- 6. Deep, prolonged unconsciousness
- 8. Obedient; docile
- 11. Make a kind of bubbling sound
- 13. Promised solemnly; pledged
- 15. Moved aimlessly and idly
- 17. Strong; healthy
- 18. Lacking clear or distinct form
- 19. Wide ditch filled with water
- 21. Outrageous
- 22. Loud outcry
- 25. Walked
- 26. Lever that steers the boat
- 27. Became less

Down
- 1. Comfortable retreat; refuge
- 3. Moving about jerkily
- 5. Soothed
- 7. Side by side
- 9. Spoke in a monotonous tone
- 10. Expressed in greater detail
- 11. See briefly
- 12. Slow in development
- 14. Slight
- 16. Impatient
- 17. Moved up quickly; swelled
- 19. Gladness
- 20. Balanced or harmonious proportions
- 23. Shapes like curves
- 24. Goad to action

VOCABULARY WORKSHEET 1 - Homecoming

___ 1. TILLER A. Unmoving; fixed
___ 2. CLAMOR B. Holding firm; stubborn
___ 3. FATIGUE C. Invading property or space of another
___ 4. CONVALESCENT D. Walk leisurely
___ 5. PURSED E. Side by side
___ 6. BICKERING F. Puckered
___ 7. CIRCUITOUS G. Weakened; became unsteady
___ 8. ABREAST H. Gathered material attached to a skirt
___ 9. IMMOBILE I. Loud outcry
___10. GLEAMED J. Squabbling; having little quarrels
___11. INTERSPERSED K. Secretly
___12. ARCS L. Shapes like curves
___13. THRONGED M. Roundabout
___14. TRUDGING N. Walking laboriously
___15. SAUNTER O. Weariness; exhaustion
___16. FLOUNCES P. Distributed randomly among
___17. FALTERED Q. Hurried along
___18. HUSTLED R. Recuperating from illness or injury
___19. TRESPASSING S. Crowded together
___20. TENACIOUS T. To one side; awry
___21. CONTRADICTORY U. Goad to action
___22. ASKEW V. Exulted loudly; boasted
___23. CROWED W. Opposite of
___24. STEALTHILY X. Lever that steers the boat
___25. PROD Y. Glowed

KEY: VOCABULARY WORKSHEET 1 - Homecoming

X - 1.	TILLER	A. Unmoving; fixed
I - 2.	CLAMOR	B. Holding firm; stubborn
O - 3.	FATIGUE	C. Invading property or space of another
R - 4.	CONVALESCENT	D. Walk leisurely
F - 5.	PURSED	E. Side by side
J - 6.	BICKERING	F. Puckered
M - 7.	CIRCUITOUS	G. Weakened; became unsteady
E - 8.	ABREAST	H. Gathered material attached to a skirt
A - 9.	IMMOBILE	I. Loud outcry
Y - 10.	GLEAMED	J. Squabbling; having little quarrels
P - 11.	INTERSPERSED	K. Secretly
L - 12.	ARCS	L. Shapes like curves
S - 13.	THRONGED	M. Roundabout
N - 14.	TRUDGING	N. Walking laboriously
D - 15.	SAUNTER	O. Weariness; exhaustion
H - 16.	FLOUNCES	P. Distributed randomly among
G - 17.	FALTERED	Q. Hurried along
Q - 18.	HUSTLED	R. Recuperating from illness or injury
C - 19.	TRESPASSING	S. Crowded together
B - 20.	TENACIOUS	T. To one side; awry
W 21.	CONTRADICTORY	U. Goad to action
T - 22.	ASKEW	V. Exulted loudly; boasted
V - 23.	CROWED	W. Opposite of
K - 24.	STEALTHILY	X. Lever that steers the boat
U - 25.	PROD	Y. Glowed

VOCABULARY WORKSHEET 2 - Homecoming

___ 1. SECLUDED   A. Loud outcry
___ 2. ELABORATED   B. Rubbed
___ 3. AMNESIA   C. Set apart
___ 4. TENDRILS   D. Frowned
___ 5. VOWED   E. Swarming
___ 6. POSTPONING   F. Despair
___ 7. CLAMOR   G. Promised solemnly; pledged
___ 8. GNAWED   H. Concentrated; firmly fixed
___ 9. MOLTEN   I. Made liquid and glowing
___ 10. CHAFED   J. Genetically transmitted
___ 11. NAUGHTY   K. Shallow trenches made in the ground by a plow
___ 12. TRAIPSED   L. Lacking clear or distinct form
___ 13. BRISKLY   M. Closed tightly
___ 14. GLEAMED   N. Mischievous
___ 15. TEEMING   O. Expressed in greater detail
___ 16. DEVOUT   P. Twisting, threadlike shoots of a plant
___ 17. CLENCHED   Q. Glowed
___ 18. SYMMETRY   R. Balanced or harmonious proportions
___ 19. FURROWS   S. In a quick, energetic way
___ 20. INTENT   T. Loss of memory
___ 21. SCOWLED   U. Walked
___ 22. VAGUE   V. Putting off until a later time
___ 23. HEREDITARY   W. Bit; chewed on
___ 24. DESPERATION   X. Deeply religious; sincere
___ 25. MOAT   Y. Wide ditch filled with water

KEY: VOCABULARY WORKSHEET 2 - Homecoming

C - 1.	SECLUDED	A. Loud outcry
O - 2.	ELABORATED	B. Rubbed
T - 3.	AMNESIA	C. Set apart
P - 4.	TENDRILS	D. Frowned
G - 5.	VOWED	E. Swarming
V - 6.	POSTPONING	F. Despair
A - 7.	CLAMOR	G. Promised solemnly; pledged
W - 8.	GNAWED	H. Concentrated; firmly fixed
I - 9.	MOLTEN	I. Made liquid and glowing
B -10.	CHAFED	J. Genetically transmitted
N -11.	NAUGHTY	K. Shallow trenches made in the ground by a plow
U -12.	TRAIPSED	L. Lacking clear or distinct form
S -13.	BRISKLY	M. Closed tightly
Q -14.	GLEAMED	N. Mischievous
E -15.	TEEMING	O. Expressed in greater detail
X -16.	DEVOUT	P. Twisting, threadlike shoots of a plant
M -17.	CLENCHED	Q. Glowed
R -18.	SYMMETRY	R. Balanced or harmonious proportions
K -19.	FURROWS	S. In a quick, energetic way
H -20.	INTENT	T. Loss of memory
D -21.	SCOWLED	U. Walked
L -22.	VAGUE	V. Putting off until a later time
J -23.	HEREDITARY	W. Bit; chewed on
F -24.	DESPERATION	X. Deeply religious; sincere
Y -25.	MOAT	Y. Wide ditch filled with water

VOCABULARY JUGGLE LETTER REVIEW GAME CLUE SHEET 1 - Homecoming

1. RDLSTIEN = 1. _____
Twisting, threadlike shoots of a plant

2. ADESXEPTERA = 2. _____
Impatient

3. GHOTNERD = 3. _____
Crowded together

4. ISLPMGE = 4. _____
See briefly

5. CIRTESEVE = 5. _____
Inclined to keeping secrets

6. EUJTOCRENC = 6. _____
Guesswork

7. LNNGGITI = 7. _____
Sparkling

8. ELTUDSH = 8. _____
Hurried along

9. ELDEAGM = 9. _____
Glowed

10. TOUDESIL =10. _____
State of being alone

11. AETRDRED =11. _____
Slow in development

12. RTYDEIHARE =12. _____
Genetically transmitted

13. SRCA =13. _____
Shapes like curves

14. CSDLEDUE =14. _____
Set apart

15. UOASCRU =15. _____
Rough-sounding; harsh

16. GIFAETU =16. _____
Weariness; exhaustion

17. DHIGYN =17. _____
Small open boat; rowboat

18. LEMONT =18. _____
Made liquid and glowing

19. GHYTAUN =19. _____
Mischievous

20. BLABED =20. _____
Splash

21. UDLLEL =21. _____
Soothed

22. BGBNOLIB =22. _____
Moving about jerkily

23. DDIDWELN =23. _____
Became less

24. LIPMYR =24. _____
Properly; precisely

25. NAUATCSYR =25. _____
Place of refuge

26. ESNTEESDIRRP =26. _____
Distributed randomly among

27. OGRDAYN =27. _____
Stiff fabric of cotton or silk

28. CONIAUTES =28. _____
Holding firm; stubborn

29. TYYESMRM =29. _____
Balanced or harmonious proportions

30. DADBOEANN =30. _____
Given up; left behind

31. GZGZIA =31. _____
Make sharp turns in alternating directions

32. DYOTCOAINRRCT =32. _____
Opposite of

33. ENEHCLDC =33. _____
Closed tightly

34. RPIENEDOATS =34. _____
Despair

35. YTAPLBUR =35. _____
Suddenly; without warning

36. EDWROC =36. _____
Exulted loudly; boasted

37. LAIDBDBE =37. _____
Obedient; docile

38. DSUREG =38. _____
Moved up quickly; swelled

39. PIDAETSR =39. _____
Walked

40. ILIOBMEM =40. _____
Unmoving; fixed

41. ESDURP =41. _____
Puckered

42. RDDENO =42. _____
Spoke in a monotonous tone

43. ILGRAEF =43. _____
Delicate; easily broken

44. LAHYEITSTL =44. _____
Secretly

45. EAKSW =45. _____
To one side; awry

46. LYIBKRS =46. _____
In a quick, energetic way

47. UOECLSFN =47. _____
Gathered material attached to a skirt

KEY: VOCABULARY JUGGLE LETTER REVIEW GAME CLUE SHEET 1 - Homecoming

1. RDLSTIEN = 1. TENDRILS
   Twisting, threadlike shoots of a plant

2. ADESXEPTERA = 2. EXASPERATED
   Impatient

3. GHOTNERD = 3. THRONGED
   Crowded together

4. ISLPMGE = 4. GLIMPSE
   See briefly

5. CIRTESEVE = 5. SECRETIVE
   Inclined to keeping secrets

6. EUJTOCRENC = 6. CONJECTURE
   Guesswork

7. LNNGGITI = 7. GLINTING
   Sparkling

8. ELTUDSH = 8. HUSTLED
   Hurried along

9. ELDEAGM = 9. GLEAMED
   Glowed

10. TOUDESIL =10. SOLITUDE
    State of being alone

11. AETRDRED =11. RETARDED
    Slow in development

12. RTYDEIHARE =12. HEREDITARY
    Genetically transmitted

13. SRCA =13. ARCS
    Shapes like curves

14. CSDLEDUE =14. SECLUDED
    Set apart

15. UOASCRU =15. RAUCOUS
    Rough-sounding; harsh

16. GIFAETU =16. FATIGUE
Weariness; exhaustion

17. DHIGYN =17. DINGHY
Small open boat; rowboat

18. LEMONT =18. MOLTEN
Made liquid and glowing

19. GHYTAUN =19. NAUGHTY
Mischievous

20. BLABED =20. DABBLE
Splash

21. UDLLEL =21. LULLED
Soothed

22. BGBNOLIB =22. BOBBLING
Moving about jerkily

23. DDIDWELN =23. DWINDLED
Became less

24. LIPMYR =24. PRIMLY
Properly; precisely

25. NAUATCSYR =25. SANCTUARY
Place of refuge

26. ESNTEESDIRRP =26. INTERSPERSED
Distributed randomly among

27. OGRDAYN =27. ORGANDY
Stiff fabric of cotton or silk

28. CONIAUTES =28. TENACIOUS
Holding firm; stubborn

29. TYYESMRM =29. SYMMETRY
Balanced or harmonious proportions

30. DADBOEANN =30. ABANDONED
Given up; left behind

31. GZGZIA =31. ZIGZAG
Make sharp turns in alternating directions

32. DYOTCOAINRRCT =32. CONTRADICTORY
Opposite of

33. ENEHCLDC =33. CLENCHED
Closed tightly

34. RPIENEDOATS =34. DESPERATION
Despair

35. YTAPLBUR =35. ABRUPTLY
Suddenly; without warning

36. EDWROC =36. CROWED
Exulted loudly; boasted

37. LAIDBDBE =37. BIDDABLE
Obedient; docile

38. DSUREG =38. SURGED
Moved up quickly; swelled

39. PIDAETSR =39. TRAIPSED
Walked

40. ILIOBMEM =40. IMMOBILE
Unmoving; fixed

41. ESDURP =41. PURSED
Puckered

42. RDDENO =42. DRONED
Spoke in a monotonous tone

43. ILGRAEF =43. FRAGILE
Delicate; easily broken

44. LAHYEITSTL =44. STEALTHILY
Secretly

45. EAKSW =45. ASKEW
To one side; awry

46. LYIBKRS =46. BRISKLY
In a quick, energetic way

47. UOECLSFN =47. FLOUNCES
Gathered material attached to a skirt

VOCABULARY JUGGLE LETTER REVIEW GAME CLUE SHEET 2 - Homecoming

1. TLEDRUSFE = 1. _____
   Made nervous or upset

2. AAESRTB = 2. _____
   Side by side

3. ESCLWDO = 3. _____
   Frowned

4. WRURSOF = 4. _____
   Shallow trenches made in the ground by a plow

5. DTOLSUE = 5. _____
   Rumpled; disheveled

6. OCTRARYN = 6. _____
   Willful; perverse; ornery

7. DLWELE = 7. _____
   Rose up

8. EONUTUS = 8. _____
   Slight

9. CHOCONPYA = 9. _____
   Jarring, discordant sound

10. UMDPLEEM =10. _____
    Beat

11. TEARELAODB =11. _____
    Expressed in greater detail

12. LHEDEE =12. _____
    Tilted

13. DRIGTU =13. _____
    Swollen

14. MEEGTIN =14. _____
    Swarming

15. NGYLODU =15. _____
    Outrageous

18. DPOR =18. _____
Goad to action

19. VONNCIICOT =19. _____
Strong belief or opinion

20. WDVEO =20. _____
Promised solemnly; pledged

21. EAVGU =21. _____
Lacking clear or distinct form

22. TUEODV =22. _____
Deeply religious; sincere

23. CDSEHLOU =23. _____
Drooped

24. TAMO =24. _____
Wide ditch filled with water

25. CNGERITI =25. _____
Repeating

26. OEMSYLNL =26. _____
Somberly; earnestly

27. NPSIGOPTNO =27. _____
Putting off until a later time

28. ESNAMIA =28. _____
Loss of memory

29. DFHEAC =29. _____
Rubbed

30. IKRICNBGE =30. _____
Squabbling; having little quarrels

31. OUMNRULF =31. _____
Causing or suggesting sadness

32. NTNITE =32. _____
Concentrated; firmly fixed

33. RAETDFEL =33. _____
Weakened; became unsteady

35. VERIEER =35. _____
State of musing; daydream

36. VEVDROEL =36. _____
Turned; rotated

37. NGRDGUIT =37. _____
Walking laboriously

38. RLTLEI =38. _____
Lever that steers the boat

39. RGGULDE =39. _____
Make a kind of bubbling sound

40. NCOOPICUUSS =40. _____
Obvious

41. OCNCOO =41. _____
Comfortable retreat; refuge

42. ITMRH =42. _____
Gladness

43. ELLUQDE =43. _____
Put down forcibly

44. RUETSNA =44. _____
Walk leisurely

45. DSCEUDCEE =45. _____
Came after

46. AEBITDVR =46. _____
Shook; trembled

47. NIPSSAGTRES =47. _____
Invading property or space of another

48. OETHSDI =48. _____
Raised; lifted

49. RALOMC =49. _____
Loud outcry

50. RDMAEEEND =50. _____
Moved aimlessly and idly

KEY: VOCABULARY JUGGLE LETTER REVIEW GAME CLUE SHEET 2 - Homecoming

1. TLEDRUSFE = 1. FLUSTERED
   Made nervous or upset

2. AAESRTB = 2. ABREAST
   Side by side

3. ESCLWDO = 3. SCOWLED
   Frowned

4. WRURSOF = 4. FURROWS
   Shallow trenches made in the ground by a plow

5. DTOLSUE = 5. TOUSLED
   Rumpled; disheveled

6. OCTRARYN = 6. CONTRARY
   Willful; perverse; ornery

7. DLWELE = 7. WELLED
   Rose up

8. EONUTUS = 8. TENUOUS
   Slight

9. CHOCONPYA = 9. CACOPHONY
   Jarring, discordant sound

10. UMDPLEEM =10. PUMMELED
    Beat

11. TEARELAODB =11. ELABORATED
    Expressed in greater detail

12. LHEDEE =12. HEELED
    Tilted

13. DRIGTU =13. TURGID
    Swollen

14. MEEGTIN =14. TEEMING
    Swarming

15. NGYLODU =15. UNGODLY
    Outrageous

18. DPOR =18. PROD
Goad to action

19. VONNCIICOT =19. CONVICTION
Strong belief or opinion

20. WDVEO =20. VOWED
Promised solemnly; pledged

21. EAVGU =21. VAGUE
Lacking clear or distinct form

22. TUEODV =22. DEVOUT
Deeply religious; sincere

23. CDSEHLOU =23. SLOUCHED
Drooped

24. TAMO =24. MOAT
Wide ditch filled with water

25. CNGERITI =25. RECITING
Repeating

26. OEMSYLNL =26. SOLEMNLY
Somberly; earnestly

27. NPSIGOPTNO =27. POSTPONING
Putting off until a later time

28. ESNAMIA =28. AMNESIA
Loss of memory

29. DFHEAC =29. CHAFED
Rubbed

30. IKRICNBGE =30. BICKERING
Squabbling; having little quarrels

31. OUMNRULF =31. MOURNFUL
Causing or suggesting sadness

32. NTNITE =32. INTENT
Concentrated; firmly fixed

33. RAETDFEL =33. FALTERED
Weakened; became unsteady

35. VERIEER =35. REVERIE
State of musing; daydream

36. VEVDROEL =36. REVOLVED
Turned; rotated

37. NGRDGUIT =37. TRUDGING
Walking laboriously

38. RLTLEI =38. TILLER
Lever that steers the boat

39. RGGULDE =39. GURGLED
Make a kind of bubbling sound

40. NCOOPICUUSS =40. CONSPICUOUS
Obvious

41. OCNCOO =41. COCOON
Comfortable retreat; refuge

42. ITMRH =42. MIRTH
Gladness

43. ELLUQDE =43. QUELLED
Put down forcibly

44. RUETSNA =44. SAUNTER
Walk leisurely

45. DSCEUDCEE =45. SUCCEEDED
Came after

46. AEBITDVR =46. VIBRATED
Shook; trembled

47. NIPSSAGTRES =47. TRESPASSING
Invading property or space of another

48. OETHSDI =48. HOISTED
Raised; lifted

49. RALOMC =49. CLAMOR
Loud outcry

50. RDMAEEEND =50. MEANDERED
Moved aimlessly and idly

www.ingramcontent.com/pod-product-compliance
Lightning Source LLC
LaVergne TN
LVHW081534060526
838200LV00048B/2078